First, humbled by your request to read and respond to your autobiography I started to read it on the Internet this morning, and I could not 'put it down' ... Frankly, your writing style with its superb flow is amazing ... And the content of your book is even more so ... What impressed me is that buoyed and guided by numerous relevant Scriptures it displays total surrender to God's sovereign and gracious ownership of everything, unquestioning obedience to His revealed will, explicit trust in His providential care, as well as ever fresh and bold undertakings to advance his Kingdom in the midst of at times 'life-threatening' circumstances. As a result it is hardly surprising that we receive the 'treat' of quite a number of impressive answers to prayer and a string of amazing triumphs in ministry. I am quite sure that this autobiography will stir and embolden thoughtful readers to strike out on their own, eager to face 'crosses' in order to end up with 'crowns'. I know it is stirring and emboldening me!

Henry Krabbendam
Professor in department of Biblical Studies, Covenant College,
Lookout Mountain, Georgia

What a story of God's grace and faithfulness! My life, too, has been intertwined in the lives of the Chinchens and the African Bible Colleges and greatly blessed through that association. My father did the initial legal work for ABC, and I prayed for and supported ABC as a seminary student and as a pastor. Then I had the privilege of speaking at the second graduation in the Macon Gym at the Malawi campus while serving as the pastor of the First Presbyterian Church in Macon, GA, which actually provided the funds for the gyms at all three ABC campuses. Later I continued my relationship with ABC as Chancellor of RTS with the US ABC offices located on our RTS Jackson campus and with many ABC students coming to RTS as well prepared seminary students who returned to their home countries in Africa as ministers. From my perspective over many years, I know of no more faithful and effective mission ministry than African Bible Colleges. This book is an inspiring story of God at work in the lives of a family willing to follow Him in faith to the ends of the earth.

Robert C. Cannada, Jr.
Chancellor and CEO
Reformed Theological Seminary,
Charlotte, North Carolina

Nell Chinchen and her husband Jack are modern-day pioneers. Life afforded them opportunity for career and comfortable living, but the Chinchens were not satisfied until they answered a higher calling. In the pages of 'A Sentimental Journey Across Africa' Nell beautifully paints a picture of what it means to recognize the providence of God, experience the leading of God, know the grace of God, and see the hand of God in every circumstance—good and bad. By putting their faith in God into action, they came to know that God's plan for Africa included not only them, but their entire family and those many that crossed their path. It has been my privilege to have a small part in their work in Liberia and to read how God guided them through the valley of trials and testing, producing a testimony worth sharing. The story of these servants of God who have been tried by fire will enlighten you and your soul will be stirred to read about the warm heart of Africa that welcomed *The Yankee Officer and the Southern Belle* with drums in the night.

Franklin Graham
President & CEO,
Samaritan's Purse,
Billy Graham Evangelistic Association

Here is the story of how God worked in the lives of two people for the extension of His Kingdom in the best and worst of times. From the refined coast of Mississippi to the shores and jungles of Africa, behold God's faithfulness to this couple and His shaping and sharpening them into instruments for His glory. Thanks be to God for the Chinchens.

Ligon Duncan
Senior Minister, First Presbyterian Church,
Jackson, Mississippi

The Mission of the Church is Missions and this book contains a heart for missions that I believe God wants found in every Christian. Wherever you find yourself, I can attest that Nell and Jack's love story for Christ, each other and the world is contagious. Once encountered and embraced it will also leave you forever changed.

Bob Botsford
Senior Pastor Horizon Christian Fellowship,
Rancho Santa Fe, California

This is definitely a 'you-can't-put-it-down' book! Just as the main characters couldn't be put down, the book itself can't be put down! From African Driver Ants in the baby's nursery to house afire in the jungle to rebel soldiers at your door, this book captures the story of 'Faith in Action, God in Motion'. Short pithy chapters, challenging adventure, and a good romance prove once more that truth can be more fascinating than fiction.

O. Palmer Robertson
Director and Principal of Africa Bible College, Uganda

The Yankee Officer and the Southern Belle is a spellbinding adventure across time and space, painting a rich tapestry of missions and the real souls touched in the making. I felt like I was transported across time to be allowed to peek in the window and catch the drama, pain, prayer, faith, and passion of a family that God has mightily used for His glory.

The Chinchen's are the real deal. The many thousands of lives that they have touched are testament to the calling that God has placed on them. Africa and the world are richer for their obedient service to our Lord. This is a must-read for all who love to see the Hand of God at work today!

John B. Sorensen
President
Evangelism Explosion International

The Yankee Officer
and
the Southern Belle

A Journey of Love across Africa

NELL ROBERTSON CHINCHEN

CHRISTIAN
FOCUS

Also available in e-book format.

© Nell Robertson Chinchen 2012

ISBN 978-1-84550-921-7

Christian Focus Publications
Published in 2012
by
Christian Focus Publications
Geanies House, Fearn,
Ross-shire, IV20 1TW, Scotland, United Kingdom

Cover design
by
Paul Lewis

Printed by
Bell and Bain, Glasgow

CONTENTS

PART I
WHERE IT ALL BEGAN – BY PROVIDENCE OF GOD

PART II
WHERE IN THE WORLD? – BY THE LEADING OF GOD

PART III
WHAT ON EARTH IS GOD DOING? – BY THE GRACE OF GOD

PART IV
WHOEVER HEARD OF LIBERIA? – BY THE HAND OF GOD

PART V
WHY US? – BY FAITH IN GOD

'Life in the Jungle' (Photo Gallery)

PART VI
WHERE DO WE STRETCH FORTH? – BY FAITH IN ACTION

PART VII
WHAT NEXT? – GOD'S PLAN FOR AFRICA INCLUDES US

DEDICATION

To My Husband –
who took my hand and led me
on this 'Sentimental Journey' across Africa

To My Children –
their wives and husbands –
who never cease to amaze me with their
commitment and accomplishments for Christ

To My Friends –
who encouraged me to write
this book, especially Connie Kay, Bob Frey,
Hermie King and so many more

To Buck and Betty Mosal –
whose prayers and sacrificial service
have helped to keep us in Africa all these years

PART I

WHERE IT ALL BEGAN – BY PROVIDENCE OF GOD

Introduction

MAGNOLIAS AND MINT JULEPS

It all began when a Yankee Officer met a Southern Belle and, in the midst of the magnolias and mint juleps, they fell head over heels in love. It was one of those wartime romances where long courtships and engagements were not possible. Actually, it was love at first sight. After a few evenings of dancing to 'Sentimental Journey' and sipping mint juleps, and of walking along the seawall of the beautiful Gulf Coast in Gulfport, Mississippi, it was no surprise when one evening that Yankee Officer in the United States Navy knelt down on the cement seawall and said bashfully, 'I don't know how I'm supposed to do this, but ... will you marry me?'

The love that began to blossom during those warm summer evenings in 1945 is the same love that carried that Yankee Officer and his Southern Belle through times of trial and testing, times of joy and sorrow, times of hardship and times of ease. But this story is not just about two people in love. This story is about what happened when a third person broke into that relationship ... a person by the Name of Jesus Christ.

1

SOUTH OF THE MASON-DIXON LINE AND THE HEATHEN WILD WEST

My Aunt Jane always said, 'What this family needs is some good red blood.' I think what she meant was that the 'blue blood' in our family was running a little thin and needed some pepping up. The family was still living on the accomplishments of our ancestors who fought valiantly in the Revolutionary War, of those who spoke out boldly for the cause of the South during the War between the States (do not DARE call it the 'CIVIL WAR' – Southerners would say there was nothing 'civil' about it) and the orations of John C. Calhoun. My mother was quite proud to point out to visitors that she had John C. Calhoun's cradle as well as his piano in our home. The closest I ever came to touching that noble figure was when I visited 'Aunt Lucia' in the old homestead near Tupelo, Mississippi. I can remember climbing up a ladder to the feather mattress on that huge four-poster bed – no doubt slept in by John C. himself. He was a great (I'm not sure how many greats) uncle. Another great uncle, (my mother's father's brother) was Andrew Kincannon, the Chancellor of the University of Mississippi. His portrait now hangs in the Mississippi Hall of Fame.

We had a coat of arms hanging in our living room that showed, without a doubt, that the Robertson clan descended from King Richard the Lionheart. I was never quite sure if this was a good thing or not, though my daddy seemed quite proud of it. He was also proud of the fact that his father gained the highest grade on his Bar exam ever made up to that time in the state of Texas. What he didn't talk about too often was the fact that my granddaddy, John Westbrook Robertson, was expelled from the University of Mississippi. It seems he went to Ole Miss with his valet and was dubbed 'The Potentate' and, being the lawyer he turned out to be, was quite outspoken. He was editor of the college paper; however, in the days before students were allowed to express their opinions too freely, he evidently wrote things he wasn't supposed to and was asked to leave, along with his valet. He ended up at Vanderbilt University. John Westbrook Robertson died fairly young. As the story goes, he was quite jealous and when my grandmother (who was Lulu Barksdale of THE Barksdales) danced with another man, my grandfather challenged him to a dual and was shot. His injury led to complications that later caused his death. So, as you can see, the Blue Blood was running a bit thin. And that's where the Heathen Wild West comes in. At least, that's what my mother called California.

When this Southern Belle met the handsome Officer in the United States Navy in Gulfport, Mississippi, and those walks on the seawall and evenings of dancing at the Broadwater Beach became too frequent for my grandmother, Lulu (whom I was visiting for the summer while I was going to Ole Miss) she called my parents in Jackson, Mississippi and told them about this 'young man from California'. They told her to put me on the bus and send me right back home! It only took a few days for me to convince my mother and daddy that they would like this 'Jack Chinchen' (What on earth kind of name is that? Chinese?) if they met him.

Reluctantly they agreed that he could come to Jackson to meet them. And he did. Being the diplomat that he is, Jack wooed my parents even as he had me! He talked sports with my dad, played tennis with my teenage brother, Jack; played card games (Battle) with my little brother, Palmer and flattered my mother's elaborately served southern dinners – only making the faux-pas of calling black-eyed peas cross-eyed peas. My parents allowed me to go back to Gulfport – on the bus with Jack!

They were still a little skeptical about his 'background', not being too sure they were ready for TOO much 'red blood!' I think it helped a little when someone in Jack's family sent my daddy a copy of *Fortune Magazine* with the major article on El Soya Ranch – a side-line recreation of some of his family. I think they began to believe that maybe what Jack had said was true – that his grandfather, John D. Crummey, started the huge corporation called, Food Machinery Corporation (FMC).

The history of that conglomerate is an incredible, rags-to-riches success story. As related in *The History of FMC* – 1884-1984, published by the FMC Corporation, San Jose, California:

> In 1863, John Bean, a lifelong inventor, came to California to retire. Royalties from past inventions allowed him to buy a ten acre almond ranch where he intended to live out the rest of his life in peace.
>
> However, a scale introduced to the area soon threatened his orchard. He bought a pump to spray his crop, but found it inadequate and inefficient. So John Bean retired to his workshop, determined to invent a pump that would deliver a continuous, steady spray rather than the irregular stream the only pump on the market offered.
>
> Bean's efforts were successful – so successful, in fact, that soon his neighbors were urging him to make sprayers for them. About this time, Bean's son-in-law David C. Crummey, visited from Wisconsin. Bean persuaded him to bring his family from Los Gatos, California, to where he could take over the pump manufacturing business. Eventually, his son, John Crummey (Jack's grandfather), quit Stanford University and joined the company. The pump they were building at that time employed a handle that worked up and down. The competitors had introduced a pump with a handle that worked back and forth. Crummey knew they had to do something to stay competitive, so he went to his grandfather and told him the type of pump they needed. The design used a vertical cylinder with a piston and a large coil spring. The new pump easily produced 120 lbs of pressure; the closest competitor could only muster 80 pounds.

John Crummey spent the next four months traveling throughout the state, demonstrating and selling the pump to enthusiastic farmers in the scale-infested areas. He soon found that the problem was not getting orders; it was filling them. There simply was not enough capital to manufacture the pumps on any large scale. So, John Crummey decided to incorporate in order to secure the much-needed funds, and he began seeking investors. As a result, the little pump business was incorporated for $15,000 and the predecessor of today's FMC was born.

The first 'MAGIC' pump offered by the company was a simple mechanism by today's standards, and it was soon followed by a succession of improved models. In 1905 the company's capitalization rose to $50,000. The company's capital doubled again in 1907. Crummey began to spend several months a year away from home as he traveled to Washington, Idaho, Utah, Colorado and Arkansas and he disliked this aspect of his work. Then something happened that he claimed affected his whole life.

He was heading home from Denver after spending Christmas away from his family. At Pueblo, an elegantly dressed man boarded the train and sat opposite Crummey. The man noticed his dejected look, and he struck up a conversation with the pump salesman. The two exchanged stories, Crummey telling of his small business, the stranger talking of his many homes. 'Gee, you must be rich,' Crummey said. 'Yes, I am,' the man said. 'Do you think you would like to trade places with me?' Crummey said he would. The man said, 'Let me tell you my story and then you can decide.'

The man told a tale of a young ambitious couple who vowed to be rich, successful socialites. Their subsequent preoccupation with business and social affairs led them to neglect their son, who proceeded to get into a variety of trouble but was saved each time by his father's money. Finally, the son, in a drunken frenzy, killed a girl and was sent to prison. The father managed two trips a year to visit his son, and it was on one of these trips that the father related this story to John Crummey.

The story made Crummey realize that no matter how pressing business was, he had to set aside some time for his children. He resolved to find time to be with his family and in later years he often stated that no amount of success equals pride in one's family.

John Crummey proved that over and over by his dedication to family affairs. After Jack and I were married, we spent many hours at the home of Grandpa and Nonna, popping pop corn on a Sunday evening, enjoying elaborate family dinners, picnics beside the waterfall at the pool and family vacations that took us all around the world. By then FMC had grown to momentous proportions and was even manufacturing the 'Water Buffalo' for the United States government. FMC built more than 11,000 amphibious landing vehicles that contributed significantly to the successful completion of the War in the Pacific.

His son-in-law, Paul Davies, who later took John Crummey's place as President of FMC and then as Chairman of the Board, had a great deal to do with the company's diversification and subsequent growth. Today FMC is still a giant in the corporate world, and it all began with a little spray pump and an eager, ambitious young man with a bicycle!

Jack's father, Samuel Arthur Chinchen, had almost the same success story. The family purchased pear orchards in the Santa Clara Valley that not only produced luscious (and lucrative) Comice pears, but also began a packing-house business called 'Sweetbrier Orchards' where Comice pears were beautifully packed and shipped all around the world, primarily at Christmas time. It was in the midst of one of these pear orchards that Jack and I built a beautiful new home in what is now known as 'Silicone Valley'. The 'Valley of Heart's Delight' was to become the heart of computer factories.

The hearts of that Yankee Officer and his Southern Belle were soon to become one in Jesus Christ. The SOUTH had joined the WEST in the greatest war of all – the war between

God and mammon. That battle was not to be won easily but we had a powerful ally, the One who is not from the South or the West, but who holds the whole world in His hand.

Nell, with Brother Jack, in front of Kincannon Hall.

2

Pear trees and Pablum

It wasn't long before the magnolias began to wilt and the mint juleps began to melt. The glamor of the white naval uniform was exchanged for blue jeans. The excitement of wartime exchanged for the monotony of living with a farmer. 'Early to bed, early to rise' was the motto. Long hours and hard work now typified our life style. Before many years the responsibility of four children dulled the remembrance of those romantic evenings. Even though money was not a problem and all our material needs were abundantly met, somehow there was an emptiness that we couldn't understand. I felt it first. It was easy for me to recognize the symptoms, having been raised in an evangelical church and having been taught the Scriptures since my early childhood. I knew I needed God back in my life.

So it was that when my little brother Palmer stepped off the train with his Bible under his arm that the search began. Palmer had come out for the summer, having just graduated from High school, to work in the pear orchards. Jack and I both noticed his dedication to Christianity right away. In California, few people attended church on Sunday evenings and very few on Wednesday evenings. And certainly NO ONE was seen with a Bible under his arm! So when Palmer faithfully attended church every time the doors were opened I became curious. One day, while he was working in the orchards, I crept into his room and STOLE his Bible! The verses began to leap out at me. 'For whoever desires to save his life will lose it, but whoever loses his life for

My sake will save it' (Luke 9:24 NKJV). Finally one day, feeling totally convicted, I decided to put all my eggs in one basket. Either the Bible was true or it wasn't. If what I was reading was true, then I knew I had to do something about it.

I suppose it was then that I made the decision to 'follow Christ.' Amazingly, soon after Palmer left to go back to Mississippi, the way opened up for me to go to a home Bible Study with Ann Brown, the wife of one of our pear-grower friends. The teachers of that Bible Study, Bill and Miriam Williamson, were converted alcoholics. I didn't know that at the time, but I do remember thinking to myself, 'If they won't let me smoke my cigarettes, I'm not going back.' Perhaps it was a little disappointing that they didn't seem to care what I did; they were only interested in what I believed. Later, I can remember how frustrated I was when I called Miriam on the phone and asked her about that smoking business. All she said was, 'Take it to the Lord.'

I took Jack with me one evening. He just had one issue (which I think he thought was unique): 'If God can send all those people to Hell who have never heard the Gospel, then I'm not interested in that kind of God.' Someone answered him with, 'Well, maybe He's calling you to be a missionary so they can hear!'

That didn't come to pass for another year, a year I spent on my knees praying and pleading with God for Jack's salvation. There were so few holes in his armor that I knew it would be difficult to penetrate his soul with God's Word. But I tried. One night, Billy Graham was being broadcast over television. Jack wasn't very happy when I asked if I could watch the Crusade. In fact, he said, 'Why do you want to listen to that fanatic?' But he didn't leave the room, even though he sat there defiantly with his newspaper before his face.

But God was beginning to answer my prayers. Strangely enough, it all began with a trip to Hawaii. Jack's parents gave us a Christmas present – a two-week trip to Hawaii – and they would even come out to the pear orchard and stay with our four children in our beautiful home. It was during one of those balmy days on the sandy beach of Hawaii that Bishop James Kennedy spotted us. Bishop Kennedy, who had once pastored the Methodist Church that Jack's family attended in San Jose, had become quite a close friend of the family. When he saw Jack, he told him he was preaching in one of the churches on the island that Sunday and that we should go to church. Jack didn't usually go but for some reason he agreed we should. Afterwards, he picked up a little devotional booklet at the back of the church. I was surprised that night as we were getting ready for bed when he said, 'Would you like me to read this to you?' He had watched me reading my Bible every night but always seemed to ignore it. That night began a ritual that was to continue after our 'second honeymoon' in Hawaii. In fact, the real honeymoon was about to begin.

On Jack's 33rd birthday I gave him his first Bible. He began reading it to me every night after we climbed into bed and soon he, too, was falling in love with Jesus Christ as the Bible began to come alive to him. Then one day, while he was pruning his young pear trees in the beautiful orchards, he dropped his pruning shears and ran into the house shouting, 'God has called me! He wants me to serve Him!' As he wrestled with this call, the words of Mark 10:29-30 kept almost leaping out of the pages!

God's promise was confirmed later when Jack's Bible kept falling open at that same passage of Scripture even as he tried to share it with his brother, Stanley! '[T]here is no one who has left house or brothers or sisters or father or mother or wife or children or lands, for My sake and the gospel's, who shall not receive a hundredfold now in this time—houses and brothers and sisters and mothers and children and lands, with persecutions—and in the age to come, eternal life.' (Mark 10:29-30 NKJV)

To me, it was an answer to my prayers. We were now ready to 'leave it all' and go to seminary. The family was not too happy about Jack deserting his post in the pear orchards and Christmas pear packing business. They threatened to cut off our income. The decision to leave our beautiful new home and the orchards and go off to seminary with four children was not an easy one, and certainly not when we knew our finances would take a dramatic downward turn.

The battle between God and mammon was, however, a minor one compared with the spiritual battle we faced at seminary. Jack's faith was tested over and over again by the seminary's professors' lack of belief in the Bible. But the more he was tested, the stronger Jack became. When he finally graduated his faith was like the Rock of Gibraltar and my knees were also hard as that rock from the many hours I had spent praying that he might not fall! Little did we know that the days of testing were not over!

PART II

WHERE IN THE WORLD? – BY THE LEADING OF GOD

3

Agates on my Windowsill

Clallam Bay was where our faith was nurtured. The impelling of the Holy Spirit that moved us out of our comfortable rut carried us through those three years of seminary. They were years when the foundations of our belief were challenged, when we learned the hard lessons of persevering in the face of ridicule and persecution, and when I especially learned the imperative of prayer. I felt like I'd spent more time on my knees than on my feet those three years, praying for Jack to be spared in that den of lions – the lions of liberalism that were waiting to devour him.

The summer between Jack's junior and senior years at seminary we were given the opportunity to minister in a small community called Clallam Bay, a remote little fishing village located on the Olympic Peninsula. It was there that God truly became alive to us. The church was made up of a handful of the local population, mostly older folks who were content with the church just as it was and had no desire to reach out to the rest of the people in that area. We soon discovered that there were loggers, schoolteachers, fishermen, resort owners, store keepers and, yes, even confirmed alcoholics that needed the Gospel. We began knocking on doors. Even though we were strangers we found that the people of Clallam Bay, as well as those living in Sekiu (a fishing village only a few miles away), were willing to ask us in and hear what we had to say. We always took one or two of our four children along with us, which probably helped to break down some of the suspicious barriers.

As we made the rounds of all the homes we came to the home of the manager of Crown-Zellerbach, the large lumber company that was located in Sekiu. The Nutters were eager to hear about our desire to begin a home Bible Study. As we left, I was praying, 'Lord, let her ask us to have the first Bible Study here in their house.' Well, she did! The next questions I asked were, 'How many pies shall I bake? How many people do you think will come?' She and I agreed on three pies, enough to serve twenty-one people. And that's exactly how many people came to our first Bible Study, a completely new concept in that non church-going community. This was a clear indication that the Holy Spirit was ready to begin a great work there. And He did!

Jack and I walked along the beach holding hands, watching the water lap against the shore, washing over the multitudes of rocks that covered the Puget Sound beach. We talked and talked of all that God was doing in Clallam Bay that summer, not wanting it to end. And we began to pray that if God wanted us to come back after Jack's graduation from seminary, He would make it clear to us.

The Clallam Bay Presbyterian Church, which had perhaps twenty people in attendance when we arrived that summer, soon began to fill to overflowing. The pastor, when he returned from his vacation, could not find a seat the first Sunday he arrived! Afterwards he said to Jack, 'I think your simplicity in preaching is appealing to these people. How would you like to come back as pastor after you graduate?' Of course, he did not recognize that what he called simplicity was the Holy Spirit giving Jack's messages the power and clarity that can only come from Him. And indeed, the people were hungry.

As we walked along those beaches in Clallam Bay and Sekiu, Jack and I often picked up the shiny, beautiful rocks, especially the agates. I took the shiniest, prettiest ones home with me and lined them up on the windowsill in the kitchen. Little did I know that those agates on the windowsill would later be a reminder of God's promise out of Isaiah, 'And I will make thy windows of agates...' (Isa. 54:12a) and that this would be the promise I needed to help me believe that God was leading us to Clallam Bay.

We were shocked one day, not long before Jack's graduation, to receive a phone call from the pastor of the Clallam Bay Church. 'I have decided not to leave,' he said. 'You cannot take this church when you graduate.' The Superintendent of the Seattle Presbytery, Dr George McCleave, called soon after that and Jack brokenheartedly told him what had happened, concluding, 'But Dr McCleave, God has called us to that church!' Dr McCleave, as a true man of God, repeated the word 'called.' 'Why,' he said, 'I haven't heard anyone use that term for years. I'm coming in on the train tomorrow to talk to you.'

Clallam Bay Presbyterian Church

My assurance to pray that we would go to Clallam Bay came from those agates on my windowsill. I had God's promise and I had begun to realize that what God promises, He will do. With the blessing of God Jack did become minister there in 1962 and, through the presence of His Spirit, that little church became a lighthouse of faith. Indeed, a separate book could be written of all the things that happened there. The little mission church supported by the Presbytery for over fifty years soon became self-supporting; the *per capita* giving to Benevolences rose from the bottom of the Presbytery list to the top and a beautiful new building was built – and our twins, Paul and Palmer were born.

Our faith grew by leaps and bounds as we watched God do one miracle after another. We were reaping the harvest of the years of prayers sowed by Nick and Marion Chesnes. This dedicated couple had witnessed and prayed for years and years, not only for the church, but for all the lost souls in that debased community. God, in His faithfulness, was now answering those prayers. And we too reaped the benefits as He increased our faith day by day. As we moved on in our service for Him, we were going to need every ounce of faith if we were to be His instruments in accomplishing His purpose for Africa. The groundwork was being laid and Jesus Christ was the cornerstone. We were being molded and equipped for a tremendous task ahead.

4

INTO THE VALLEY

I shouldn't call it the valley of despair, but in many ways it was just that to me. Someone once said that the more God blesses us, the harder it is to give up those blessings to follow Him. Clallam Bay was everything I had ever longed for. The church was growing; the Women's Bible Study I was teaching was exciting as I opened up God's Word to many who had never really heard it before. I loved hearing Jack preach Sunday after Sunday. And the beautiful beaches overflowing with shiny agates were always there for us to walk together and rejoice over what God was doing in the lives of these people we had come to love and appreciate.

Jack's burden for Christian education was evident long before it became a popular topic among Christians. Our friend and Bible teacher from San Jose, Dave Wallace, had started a small Christian school in a church in Los Gatos, California. It was growing so rapidly that he wanted to build a 'real' Christian High School for that metropolis and he wanted Jack to come back to the Valley and help him get the property and raise money for the high school.

To me it was like a voice of doom. I had so many questions. Should Jack give up the pastorate for which I had prayed so passionately? Was it time to leave Clallam Bay? Seven years of watching God work in people's lives did not seem long enough! Going back to where we started seemed almost like a retreat! I was exactly like Jonah. I didn't know then that God had souls there He wanted to hear the message of salvation and He needed to prepare us for what was ahead.

The finding of the property for Valley Christian High School was but a small part of God's job for us. Jack had the goal of raising $100,000 as a down payment for the land. We prayed, and he spoke in churches, yet nothing seemed to happen. One day, after reading Reese Howells' book *Reese Howells, Intercessor*. I said, 'We can't ask others to give until we give what we can.' So together we took what we had in stocks and bonds and sold them for $50,000. Within the week, the rest of the money was in and Valley Christian High School was on the way to becoming a reality.

Remember, in Genesis, God comforted Leah by giving her a child. He did the same for me! It was during these days of being in the Valley that He blessed us with another daughter, Marion Susan. Marion has brought sunshine into our lives ever since.

But it was also during this time that we realized our son, Vann had a passion for automobiles. Occasionally he would 'borrow' one for a joyride. There was one time when we became aware that he had one such car parked down the street from our house. Even though I was expecting Marion Susan, Jack and I got up early the next morning and PUSHED that car down to the nearest gas station. Vann never said anything but I am sure he was more than surprised when he went out to take a spin in 'his' car!

It was also during this time that Bill Clark reappeared into our lives. We had become acquainted with the Clarks while pastoring the church in Clallam Bay. They were running a Camp in Poulsbo, Washington called 'Island Lake Bible Camp'. Bill let the word out that he needed some help from the men in the surrounding churches in laying floor tiles in the dining room of the Bible Camp. Jack drove over one Saturday to lend a hand and he and Bill hit if off immediately. Bill was a great prayer warrior and the pair of them spent more time on their knees praying than laying tile! So it should have been no surprise when, after Bill had spoken in chapel at Valley Christian School, he came to our home in Los Gatos and asked us to go up to the Camp for the summer and manage the Day Camp program.

While Jack seemed interested in Bill's proposal, I was flabbergasted! Our baby was due in August! I said, 'Absolutely not!' But Jack answered with the, 'Where's your faith?' line that has become the byline for this family! After many tears and prayers the Lord did convince me that this was what he wanted us to do. The fact that Marion would be born in the same hospital in Port Angeles as the twins, and that I would have Dr John Seimens, who had delivered the twins, as my doctor, certainly made the decision easier. That we would be able to spend three weeks after the baby was born with Marion and Nick Chesnes was an added bonus, even if we did have to put Marion Sue in a dresser drawer because her beautiful bassinet was in Los Gatos! That summer turned out to be a blessing for all of us. The twins learned how to ride horses; Del was able to be a counselor and Lisa enjoyed all the activities of a Bible Camp. Our friendship with the Clarks later led them to become missionaries to Africa and to take our place at ENI (Elizabeth Native Interior) Mission in Liberia when we went on furlough for a year.

God's providence never ceases to amaze me. His ways truly are past finding out. The hard part is to be obedient to His leading even when we can't see where we are going. An old song says, 'Just round the corner there's a rainbow in the sky'. But there's more than a rainbow, there's a pot of gold. His 'treasure map' is in His Word and His providence will lead us there. Sometimes, however, the times of testing are also our times of preparation. That Valley of Despair in the Valley of Heart's Delight was our training ground for providing educational institutions in the continent of Africa. It was just another step in the direction in which He was leading us.

5

The pepper bird beckons

Picayune may mean 'small' but it certainly is not insignificant. One step at a time is how God leads us and a step might be small. But each step is a stepping stone laid by His hand of providence.

After the twins were born, while we were still in Clallam Bay, Jack and I both decided it was time to visit my family in Mississippi. We knew it would be expensive to fly our entire family clear across the United States. In those days people did not jump on an airplane at the drop of a hat as they do today! So, as we always did when making an important decision, we began to pray about it. We took out our savings and, sure enough, we had exactly the amount of money we needed for the trip. Somehow, though, neither one of us had complete peace of mind that this was the right time to go.

As we prayed and sought the Lord's will in this, we decided that the only way we would be certain we were making the right decision was to give all that money away and wait and see if the Lord Himself provided what we needed for the plane fare. That decided, we sat down and wrote checks to Billy Graham and Bill Bright's Campus Crusade and then we waited to see what God would do.

When the time came for us to leave Clallam Bay for the summer, we drove as far as San Jose, California, to visit Jack's family. There we waited ... and waited, each day expecting the money for those tickets. Nothing came. Finally it was time to go back to Clallam Bay. But before we left – as we were all packed in the car – we checked the mail one last time. There we found a check for the exact amount we needed! But it was too late. Or was it?

No, it wasn't. The following spring my brother, Palmer called and asked Jack to come to Picayune to preach a series of evangelistic messages at The First Presbyterian Church of Picayune, where he was pastor. God's providence was opening the way for Jack to be called to that church just a few years later as pastor. And it was from Picayune that God called us to Liberia.

We were preparing for the church's first Missionary Conference and the more we focused on missions, the stronger became our own desire to 'GO YE'! God began to speak to me out what we know as 'the Great Commission' – Mark 16:15, 'Go ye into all the world and preach the Gospel ...' Meanwhile Jack was reading a book by Norman Lewis called, **Go Ye Means YOU**. He had also been preaching through Matthew and his sermon, 'Our going hurries His coming', taken from Matthew 24:14, was one he would use over and over to encourage OTHERS to go to the mission field. The disciples had asked Jesus, '[W]hen will these things happen, and what *will be* the sign of your coming?' (Matt. 24:3 NASB). Jesus answered, '[T]his gospel ... shall be preached in the whole world as a testimony to all nations and then the end shall come' (Matt. 24:14 NASB). Both of us agreed that we were being 'called' to the mission field.

The confirmation of our call came with the arrival of our Mission Conference speaker. Paul Chang, who represented Christian National Evangelism Commission (CNEC), stayed in our home. On the first morning after his arrival, while we were having breakfast, he asked Jack, 'What did you do before God called you into the ministry?' Jack answered, 'I used to be a fruit grower in California.' Paul replied excitedly, 'God could use you in Liberia!' He went on to explain. 'I have just been at the CNEC Headquarters in San Jose, California, and Gus Marwieh, the Director of the CNEC mission in Liberia, was pleading for us to send someone who had both pastoral and agricultural experience. Gus has been given the responsibility

of training over one hundred pastors who are working with the
Le Tourneau Foundation to establish churches in South Liberia.
It seems Le Tourneau has closed down their work in Liberia but
these newly appointed pastors still need to be trained.' Paul went
on to explain that Gus also had a burden for agriculture. Jack
fitted the combination!

Of course, we had reservations. It was a big decision. I even
had a lot of excuses as to why we should NOT go. First of all,
I felt Jack, at forty-five, was too old. Then there was the fact
that we had seven children (I didn't know any missionary with
that many children!). But my most pressing excuse of all was
that Jack was a good preacher and maybe he should just stay
here and preach and send other YOUNG people to the mission
field. But then I remembered something Reese Howells said in
his book, **Reese Howells, Intercessor**. 'You can never ask others
to do what you yourself are not willing to do.' So, certain that
God would not take us up on our offer, we got down on our
knees and said, 'Lord, we're willing.' That was when the call
came to go to Liberia.

As I had never heard of this little country before, I went down
to the public library in Picayune and began to read everything
I could find about Liberia. One of the books, **The Land of the
Pepper Bird**, gave incredible insights but discouraging information. It seemed as though this was probably the worst place in
the whole world to live! It was hot, it was humid; the water was
so contaminated that you couldn't drink it and there were so
many diseases it had been called 'the white man's grave.' Not
only that, there were lots of snakes, and I didn't like snakes!
I had second thoughts about that call to Liberia!

The next Sunday, however, Jack was preaching on Mark 16
and, following the familiar, 'Go ye…' of verse 14, he noted that
God has given some amazing promises. 'In My name they will
cast out demons; they will speak with new tongues; they will
take up serpents; and if they drink anything deadly, it will by
no means hurt them; they will lay hands on the sick, and they

will recover' (NKJV). There were the three things that I was the most concerned about. I believed those promises and was ready to face the challenge of a new and strange land.

So it was at the close of that Missions Conference at the First Presbyterian Church in Picayune, Mississippi, when the invitation was given for those to come forward who felt led of God to go to the mission field, a very surprised congregation watched their pastor and his wife and children walk down the aisle, hand in hand, to answer that call. And they were not alone. The congregation graciously gave up their Sunday evening services in order that their pastor could travel to other churches, raising the financial and prayer support needed for such a huge step of faith. They, too, believed Matthew 24:14 and desired to be a part of 'hurrying His return'.

Today that verse is printed at the bottom of the African Bible Colleges' stationery. 'And this gospel of the kingdom will be preached in all the world as a witness to all the nations, and then the end will come.' It stands as a reminder of why, after all these years, we (and many of our children) are still here!

PART III

WHAT ON EARTH IS GOD DOING? – BY THE GRACE OF GOD

6

Stepping into the Unknown

The manse was empty; the boxes all packed and loaded in the moving van. My brother Palmer had come with a U-Haul truck to take our Chippendale living room furniture to Jackson to put in his house at Reformed Theological Seminary where he was teaching. Little did we know then that 20 years later he would ship some of that same furniture to the Bible College in Malawi where he and his wife would be teaching! I like to think of it as 'bread cast on the waters.' As we sat on the floor in the vacant living room, surrounded by some of the saints from the Presbyterian Church in Picayune, and prayed, I knew then that 'surely the Lord is in this place', (Gen. 28:16) and that His promise to Jacob was to us too, 'I will be with you and keep you.'

Everything was ready as we piled little Marion Sue, Paul, Palmer and Lisa into our station wagon. We planned to spend Christmas with Jack's family in California and then to see Delbert in Washington State before flying to Canada to speak in the great People's Church in Toronto and to meet with Oswald Smith. In memory of his wife, Oswald Smith had given the money to build a training school for pastors in the middle of the jungle of Liberia at ENI Mission. From there we would fly out to New York and then on to Africa – the place that God had written on my heart.

We did have one problem. We had no visas to allow us entry to Liberia. The organization we were going out under had never sent missionaries before; hence we had very little information on the proper procedures. We had applied for visas, sent in our passports to the Liberian Embassy in Washington, D.C. and waited for everything to be mailed back to us. But when the time of our departure came, the visas had not arrived. I frantically called the Embassy in Washington and they very calmly said that we should simply leave our next address with them and they would send the visas and passports there.

That certainly sounded reasonable enough. So, without any reservations whatsoever, we headed out for San Jose, California. However, when we arrived at Jack's parents' home there was no sign of any of the documents. Once again I called the Embassy and reminded them that we were leaving for Liberia soon and needed the passports and visas immediately. Once again they replied calmly that the documents would be waiting for us at our next destination in Washington State.

This time, I admit, I was somewhat concerned. But God in His grace gave us assurance. As we drove to Washington State I read to Jack from a little New Testament I carried in my purse. I was surprised to find a verse written on the flyleaf of that little Bible 'As thou goest, thy way shall be opened up … step by step …. Before thee' (ancient Hebrew version Prov. 4:12).

God, in His marvelous way of making His will known, was telling us to 'keep going'. And we did. Fully expecting that the visas would be waiting for us in Washington, we were totally surprised when we arrived and asked for our mail and once again there was nothing! Another call to the Liberian Embassy reassured us that everything was in order and the documents would be … without fail … at the People's Church waiting to be picked up. On the strength of Proverbs 4:12, we kept going. The first thing we did after the plane landed in Toronto, Canada was to drive straight to the Church office, with the intention of picking up our visas, only to be informed that nothing had arrived for the Chinchens!

Time was running out. Knowing the offices would be closed over the weekend, I wasted no time in once again calling the Liberian Embassy. 'Where are the visas?' I asked. 'Oh, Mrs Chinchen, don't worry. Everything will be waiting for you at

New York Airport.' Only that verse from Proverbs could have encouraged us to keep moving. On Monday morning we flew into J.F.K. Airport in New York and literally ran to find the proper desk where our passports and visas were supposed to be waiting. Somewhat out of breath we asked, 'Do you have something from the Liberian Embassy for us?' 'Sorry,' was the reply, 'there is nothing here.'

Jack and I looked at each other, not believing what we heard. Now what? Go back home? We knew we couldn't get into Liberia without visas. With his usual undaunted determination, Jack said, 'I'm taking a helicopter to Washington, D. C. to get those visas. You go ahead and check the bags in.' We didn't know it then, but that was the beginning of the motto for African Bible Colleges, 'Faith in action – God in motion.' Didn't Proverbs 4:12 say 'As thou goest …'

Off Jack went. As soon as the helicopter landed in Washington, D.C., he hopped into a taxi and went straight to the Liberian Embassy, bounded up the steps and threw open the door to their office. When they saw him the people working in the office said, 'Oh, Rev. Chinchen, we're so glad you're here. You can help us finish filling out these visa forms!' That was our introduction to Liberia – the laid-back, never-in-a-hurry lifestyle that we were to come to love and appreciate. But right then Jack was in a hurry! As the PanAm flight to Monrovia, Liberia was leaving early that evening, Jack helped them get everything in order quickly and flew back to New York. I had already checked in our 21 suitcases, and the children and I were standing in line to the plane when Jack triumphantly joined us with a big smile on his face! Another victory for Jesus!

Only later did we realize how important it was that we be on that plane. Waiting on the other side of the Atlantic was a multitude of people. Some had walked for two days to get out of the jungle and then had taken money-buses, and had even slept at the airport, in order to greet us as we arrived in Liberia! So it was that when our plane touched the ground we looked out the window and saw people dancing and singing. We asked,

'Who is the V.I.P. on this plane?' We didn't realize that they were waiting for US until we got off the plane and were completely enveloped in the loving arms of these tribal people who had waited for so long for someone to come and live among them and teach them the Gospel of our Lord Jesus Christ. Colorful garments were placed over our heads. The children were picked up and the little ones tied on the backs of the ladies with their 'lappas'. Songs were sung, speeches given and love in abundance bestowed upon us. We have often said, 'What if?' 'What if we had not kept going?' 'What if we had turned back?'

On the plane that morning, just as the sun was coming up in West Africa, Jack and I had our devotions and read from the devotional book *Streams in the Desert* by L.B. Cowman. The devotional for January 6 was a confirmation that we had done the right thing. It read like this: 'When you pass through the waters, I will be with you; and when you pass through the rivers, they will not sweep over you' (Isa. 43:2 NIV).

'God does not open paths for us before we come to them, or provide help before help is needed. He does not remove obstacles out of our way before we reach them. Yet when we are at the edge of our need, God's hand is outstretched. Many people forget this truth and continually worry about difficulties they envision in the future. They expect God to open and clear many miles of road before them, but He promises to do it STEP BY STEP only as their need arises. You must be IN the flood waters before you can claim God's promise.'

God told Abraham to 'Go to a place that I will show you,' and we read in Hebrews chapter eleven that 'Abraham went to a place that he knew not ...' He didn't know where he was going, but he knew he was going where God wanted him to go. And so it was with us. We had to just keep going, trusting that God was going to open the way for us. And He did.

Liberia was our unknown, and we were stepping into the unknown ... by faith. And it was by faith, enveloped in total darkness, that we followed the people that night to a small church with a tin roof by the water's edge. As we trudged through the sandy soil, having no idea where we were going, we felt completely safe and secure. The Gbaizon tribe and the Kru tribe had prepared a welcome service for us at this little church and, as we listened to song after song and welcome speeches and prayers for us, we felt very privileged to be so loved. When we were given the opportunity to speak, the twins and I shared a song that seemed very appropriate for the occasion.

As the pastor of the church introduced us we had our first glimpse of the fact that Liberians are 'people watchers' for he proudly told the congregation, 'Since these children have entered the church they have not left the side of their parents. They have not been running around the church. You see now?'

After I said the words carefully for the interpreter, Paul, Palmer and I sang:

Faith is just believing
What God says he will do.
He will never fail us,
His promises are true.

If you but receive Him
His children you become.
Faith is just believing
His wondrous work is done.

Gus Marwieh gave his welcome speech, including in it the story of a recent visit to the Vice-President's home. He related in detail how graciously he and his choir were received by Dr and Mrs Tolbert (later to become President of Liberia). We left the church and began the walk back through the sandy beach. Some of the women picked up the twins and Marion Sue and placed them on their hips. Then, taking off their lappas, (the colorful cloth worn by Liberian women and used for a multitude of purposes) they wrapped them around the children like slings and carried them on their backs. I couldn't help but be amazed at how the twins accepted all these strange happenings. God had given them to us for just this purpose – to open the hearts of the people to these strangers from a far off land. Actually, our four little children were the keys that turned the locks of many hardened hearts later on as we lived our lives like an open book in our bamboo house in the jungles of Liberia. The unknown was seemingly the known to them. There were never any tears or cries of 'Why have you brought us to this strange place?' because it was home to them right from the beginning.

PART IV

WHOEVER HEARD OF LIBERIA? – BY THE HAND OF GOD

Liberia – I love you!

The motto for the country of Liberia is 'The love of liberty brought us here.' My motto as a missionary to Liberia could be 'The love of Liberia brought me here!'

I wrote this poem before we ever went to Liberia,

Liberia, I love you

Liberia, I love you;
  though I have not touched your shores,
  my heart has crossed the ocean
  and lodged within your door.

Liberia, I love you;
  you were written in my heart
  before I ever knew you
  or longed this Gospel to impart.

Liberia, I love you;
  my God, he loves you too,
  and the Christ that died for me
  died for Liberia too.

Liberia, I love you;
  this is your golden hour,
  the time has come, the time is now
  for you to know God's power.

Liberia, I love you;
  and this message that I bring
  will turn your heart to Jesus
  and will make the angels sing!

7

A SENATOR ON THE STREET CORNER

The providence of God never ceases to amaze me. When we were ushered into the Dukor Hotel, located on the top of the highest hill in Monrovia, we were a little disappointed at all the luxury that surrounded us. We thought we were going straight to the bush of Liberia and we were eager to get to our new home. But next morning Gus Marwieh gave us the disheartening news that we would not be able to get our residence visas until all our educational documents arrived from the States. No one had told us that this would be necessary and it would have been easier to write to our various colleges and seminary for degree certificates and transcripts while we were still in the United States than to try to communicate from Africa. We knew that could take weeks and weeks! Remember, this was in the days before e-mail and a reliable telephone service. We needed help.

As Gus Marwieh, Jack and I knelt around the bed in our hotel room, Gus lifted up his voice to God in a powerful plea for help. We had just finished reading in Proverbs 16:3: 'Commit thy works unto the Lord, and thy thoughts shall be established.' Gus committed our works unto the Lord. He called upon God to intervene so we could be allowed to go up country to Sinoe County without the proper documents and to wait there for them instead of having to stay in Monrovia.

We, of course, knew little about Liberia's immigration rules at that time. And I doubt if Gus did either, not ever having had to deal with missionaries before. A short time later, as we stepped out of the hotel and started walking toward the

Education Building, a big impressive car pulled up on the curb, almost running us over. Out jumped a gentleman in a black suit, obviously someone of importance. He threw his arms around Gus, greeted us and told us to get into his limousine. 'Who is this man?' I wondered. Gus turned excitedly to us and proudly introduced Senator Harrison Grigsby, Senator from Sinoe County. We learned later that he was more than just a senator; he was very respected in the political structure of Liberia.

When we told Senator Grigsby what we were required to do, he immediately went with us to all the necessary government offices, cut through the red tape and, in just a few hours, obtained permission for us to proceed to ENI Mission. In Exodus, God told Moses, 'I send an Angel before you to keep you in the way and to bring you into the place which I have prepared' (Exod. 23:20 NKJV).

I think there are a lot of angels in Africa. That may be because we needed them more there as we were always venturing out into unknown situations. In any case, God never leaves us desolate. Even in the most difficult situations. He always providentially provides the help we need – sometimes just in the nick of time! Once again God had given us a verse, we had claimed it in prayer, and our works had been accomplished.

Senator Grigsby and his wife became two of our closest friends over the years. He always stood by to give us the advice, the counsel and the presence we needed to get things accomplished. It was he who drew up the constitution for African Bible College – Liberia, and took it before the Senate and House of Representatives for approval.

Once again, God had given us a verse, we had claimed it in prayer, and our works had been established.

8

DRUMS IN THE NIGHT

The next few days were spent in Monrovia making preparations for jungle living. We knew we would have to take in supplies but we also knew there was no road into the mission station. The little Cessna 180 aircraft that would be our lifeline could only carry a few passengers, certainly not the load of groceries we would need for months! Once again we consulted Senator Grigsby. As the Senator had been the head of the armed forces, he immediately said he could supply us with an army jeep and a trailer that could carry the things we needed over the fourteen hours of rough roads to Sinoe County. Great! I was ready to go!

Before Gus Marwieh had left for ENI Mission, however, he told Jack that the house the people were building for us was not yet ready. Jack felt that he needed to fly into the mission station first and check it out (spy out the land!) before he took his whole family into an unknown situation. I wasn't convinced this was a good idea but there was no way I could talk him out of it. Off he went into the wide blue yonder. The missionary pilot Bud Heinzeg picked him up at the airport in Greenville and began the dangerous flight over the thickest forest in all of Africa. Then began the search for the clearing and the small hidden airstrip – only 750 feet long – where he could drop the little Cessna 180 down between the trees.

Bud landed his plane and immediately buzzed off leaving Jack standing all alone on the airstrip. Right on the very edge of the airstrip was our bamboo house. Gus was right; it wasn't finished. There were no doors and no windows or screens. But the house had been very carefully built up on stilts for protection against wild animals roaming about. And the matting of the house was beautifully painted a bright green and white. I fell in love with it the moment I saw it. All the other houses were mud block with dirt floor; this was truly a luxurious dwelling place, lovingly prepared for us by the people we had come to serve.

But as Jack looked about at the somewhat desolate mission station, with its tin buildings and houses made with blocks of mud, then at our future home without windows and doors to protect against mosquitoes and other invaders, he felt like those spies that crept into the Promised Land. His heart melted with fear. That fear gripped him hard that night as he lay on a small cot in the open house and listened to the chanting and beating of drums from the nearby village. He told me later that he cried and asked God, 'How can I bring my family out here to the middle of this jungle?'

Jack knew later that that trip was a mistake. It is always a mistake to spy out the land ahead of time. Missionaries who go to see if they will like it never do. God just doesn't pour out His Grace for such a venture. He withholds His grace for the time we mean business, for the time we are committed to His Call – no matter what.

And I was committed to Africa. I had taken everything I needed to make a home. It was all in a container on the ocean and would wait until Jack could cut a six mile road through the jungle to bring it in. Then I could really set up housekeeping! I had even shipped my Van Gogh painting and my cherry bedroom set. But in the meantime, we had cots and hammocks and a door not yet set up that we used for a dining room table.

Flying into that jungle was the most wonderful experience I have ever had in my life. The Jungle is beautiful. As we flew for the first time over the thick forest, the densest jungle in all of Africa, it took my breath away. The tall trees so meshed together that it looked like one huge carpet of green. Occasionally there was a small opening and we could glimpse a village with thatched roofs pointing skyward like upside down ice cream cones. But other than those few scattered clearings, God's handiwork was virtually undisturbed. I felt as though I had entered into a world that was untarnished by human hands, a world that was fresh and new yet centuries old.

As our little Cessna 180 set down on the short airstrip we were not sure what to expect. All we knew was that the people had been working hard preparing the house for us and had started cutting a road through the forest in order that we would not be so isolated. We had a sense of expectation that can only come when venturing into the unknown, knowing that the unknown is known by God and we are completely in His hands!

As soon as the plane touched the ground we were enveloped by the welcoming multitude of people. They quite literally swept us up in their arms and lifted us up on their shoulders. Hammocks, resting on the heads of four men, were rushed to the plane and the twins and Lisa were put into one while Marion Sue and I were lifted into the other one! She immediately started to cry in the midst of all the confusion but we were soon bouncing away down the jungle trail to the nearest village, Plantibalibo. As the people sang and chanted and danced in front of us I was filled with an emotion too overwhelming to describe. A combination of great joy at being welcomed so warmly and fear that we would not live up to their expectations. I wanted so desperately to be a good missionary! Little did I know that the next seven years were to test that desire to the uttermost.

That night, as I entered a jungle paradise, the drums in the night were just a reminder of the thousands of Liberians out there in that forest who had never heard the good news of Jesus Christ.

9

ENI MISSION

ENI Mission (Elizabeth Native Interior) was brought into being by the daughter of a freed slave, 'Mother George', as she was called by all the tribal people. 'Eliza' arrived in Liberia when she was 40 years old and when her attempts to start a school in the coastal town of Greenville failed, a young man by the name of Otto Klibo insisted she come deeper into the interior where there was a dire need for education. He promised to help clear the forest and build enough buildings to begin a mission station with a primary school for the children from the nearby village of Plantibalibo and even more remote villages across the river.

Eliza Davis George came to Liberia in January 1914. She lived in Bassa for five years and it was there that she met her husband, an American engineer who had dedicated his life to Christ at the grave of Mrs David Livingston, saying, 'If she, an alien, could give her life for my people, there's nothing less that I can do. I, too, must follow her path.'

After he died, Mother George continued the work in Sinoe County. The small Christian school was a continuous challenge. Trying to find clothes for some 50 children was so difficult that she would often give up her own clothes, keeping only what she was wearing, in order for the children not to be naked. Gus Marwieh, who later became the director of ENI Mission, arrived at the school one day at the age of 14 with no clothes. When told he had to have something to wear, he went back to his village and borrowed his cousin's bubba (blouse). At night he returned it to her and borrowed it again for the next day's classes at the mission school.

Right from the beginning it was obvious to Mother George that young Marwieh had potential as a Christian leader. It was not long before his zeal for the things of Christ became evident and he made clear to everyone his burden for the lost souls around him. In a letter he expressed this strong yearning for others to become concerned for his people:

> Missionaries have been sent to people who sat in darkness and did not know the tragedy of their plight. They resisted all efforts until sovereign grace overcame stubbornness against the light.
>
> I have been called to a race of men and women who sit in darkness and know the true nature of their condition. They have too long sought for a change with the passion of a thirsty soul walking up and down in an arid desert in search of a cool drink.
>
> Let me remind you that a man who has gone for many days without eating food has a very special flavor that a routine eater has not tasted in all his eating and he will never taste until he experiences the craving of the body cells, the tissues, the nerves and all the vital parts of the body when they are denied the use of food upon which he depends for survival.
>
> Remember that the Word of God could never taste the same to the Jews of Thessalonica, Derbe or Lystra as it did taste to the people of Macedonia. The cry is still, 'Come Over and Help Us.'
>
> Please permit me to share with you from the heart a burden that has often caused hot tears to well up in my eyes and run down my checks like water. We have minds but they have not been developed. We have souls but they are in need of cleansing. We have energies but they are misdirected.
>
> We have children but it breaks our hearts to see their little bodies wasted by malnutrition and the most formative years of their lives wasted away and passed forever with nothing left to challenge the mind. We have bodies but they puzzle us greatly, for they are not exactly well, neither are they exactly sick so they keep us painfully in doubt as to the direction which the

compass of our lives is pointed. We have man power, but who can harness it for us. We have land but it lies in waste. We have raw materials but we know not their values.

We have been here since the beginning of the human race but we have not yet caught up with people who lived in the age of the horse and buggy. So, late in this twentieth century we have not yet learned the use of the wheel. We are almost ready to cry like Jeremiah 'the summer's past, the harvest is ended, and we are not saved'. (Augustus Marwieh, 1969)

Indeed, it was no surprise that this one who began his education at the age of 14 was later sent to Simpson Bible College in the United States to continue his education and then to the University of California to receive a Master's Degree. Nor was it surprising that he would be chosen along with thirty-nine other outstanding alumni of the University of California to participate in an autobiography of the University during the years 1869 to 1969 entitled, *There Was Light*.

When God called us to this remote mission station in the middle of the jungles of Liberia, we had the privilege of working with, and learning from, Augustus B. Marwieh, a protégé of Mother George. Those seven years at ENI Mission were our training ground, our boot camp for the battle which lay ahead.

10

COMING HOME

Crossing the Mason-Dixon Line into the Heathen Wild West was a lot more difficult for me than crossing the ocean and entering into that 'glorious land of liberty' – Liberia. Going into that little country was like turning back the pages of history to where the Old South began. To me, it was like 'coming home'. Nothing was strange.Later, after we started the Bible Colleges and I taught, Cultural Anthropology, I learned that 'culture shock' is often a problem new missionaries face. I wasn't expecting any such thing and it never happened. Mainly because the culture in which I was brought up and the culture of Liberia were so similar.

The mission station where we were located was about fifty miles from Greenville, named after a town in Mississippi. There was also a Mississippi Street. Even the names of the people in those coastal towns sounded like names I had heard all my life. This should have been no surprise since Liberia was settled by freed American slaves. The majority of these settlers were from the state of Mississippi. The American Colonization Society was formed to help freed slaves go back to their 'roots'. Most of those who went back were Christians, and they went with the hope of evangelizing their own people. As it turned out the jungle was too thick, and the forest so dense, that most of these freed slaves settled along the coast.

Monrovia (named for President James Monroe) became the capital and a constitution was drawn up. It was patterned after the Constitution of the United States of America, with a Senate and a House of Representatives. The men, as befitted gentlemen from the Old South, wore top hats and tails and the ladies always dressed elegantly; they still do today. Their houses were built, as much as possible, to look like the southern mansions to which they had been accustomed. But sometimes, for lack of other building materials, tin sheeting was used for the exterior. Many of them, however, had taken stained glass windows back with them so these were very prevalent, especially in the homes in Buchannan. Our daughter-in-law, Becky, was later able to acquire some of that beautiful stained glass to put in their home in Yekepa.

A friend of ours in Natchez, Mississippi had access to letters in the Library of Congress that freed slaves had written to their former masters. She gave me copies of some of these and I used them in my thesis on *The History of Education in Liberia*. These slaves were obviously well educated and all made reference to their faith in God.

The motto of Liberia is 'The love of liberty brought us here.' But I think that it was the love of God that inspired them to make such a sacrifice. And it was a sacrifice. As the letters of those first settlers indicated, it was not easy. There was much suffering and sickness. Malaria, yellow fever and dysentery took their toll. Planting farms, building houses and attempting to establish a new nation was extremely difficult. The heat, the humidity and the heavy rains during the rainy season all made survival in this strange country a challenge. But the settlers were persevering, God-fearing people.

The Constitution was drawn up, a President appointed and a nation was born. That nation was so stable and steadfast that for 150 years it was the only Christian democracy in the entire world other than the United States of America. That Christian democracy still stands today although there have been wars, coups, countercoups and rebel incursions. Miraculously the solid rock of Christianity and the original Constitution still stand today.

No, culture shock was never a factor in our move from Mississippi to Liberia; we simply changed our address. And the love that God placed in my heart before we ever left home in the States continued to grow and envelop the multitudes of people that crowded around that little bamboo house day after day. The Psalmist says, 'In thy presence is fullness of Joy', (Ps. 16:11) and also in the familiar 23rd Psalm we read, 'My cup runneth over.' (Ps. 23:5)

There was no doubt about it. I had come HOME.

11

FIREFLIES IN MY BEDROOM

Pegboard walls in our bedroom gave the impression that a thousand eyes were looking at us. Of course, no one could really see through those tiny holes in the walls, but they did make it possible for the fireflies to bring their shimmering lights into that dark room. Sometimes there would be so many of those flickering little bugs flying around that they would actually light up the darkness. With no electricity and few kerosene lanterns I honestly thanked the Lord that someone had the foresight to build the bedroom with pegboard walls.

In fact, everything designed for that bamboo house was just about perfect. I know Cecelia Marwieh (Gus Marwieh's wife, who had been selected for him by Mother George) had a great deal to say about how the house was built. It was actually a first of its kind. All the houses in Plantibalibo, and those on the ENI Mission, were made out of mud blocks with dirt floors and thatched roofs. They had no paint, no windows and no inside kitchen. This house was unique. The woven mat walls that made up the exterior of the house were painted a colorful green and white. Even the inside ceiling was painted bright green and white and a beautiful pattern woven in the bamboo matting. In fact, when Al Finley, the Director of CNEC (Christian Nationals Evangelism Commission) visited us and I was telling him how Jack's grandmother, Caroline Crummey didn't like us living in the jungle in a bamboo house, he said, 'Maybe she forgot to look up.' By that he meant she didn't see the beauty that surrounded us.

Of course, there were a few things about the house that took a bit of adjusting. For instance, the door into our bedroom was made to fit the downward slant of the house. This meant that every night we had to bring down an extra piece of wood to fill in the gap between the door and the floor or else the rats would scamper into the room and even bounce over our bed. The only problem with that solution was that when Marion Sue woke up at night and cried for her bottle, I had first to lift up the wood, find the kerosene lantern, and then hesitantly make my way to the kitchen, all the while hoping I wouldn't meet one of those rats along the way.

The rats were a minor threat compared to the voracious driver ants. The first time we were invaded by these little flesh-eating creatures, I wasn't really aware of how dangerous they could be. That particular night Paul and Palmer were the first ones to be alerted. They had put our chimpanzee, Sadi-Ju to sleep in a small box next to their beds. But in the middle of the night Sadi-Ju began screeching in that high pitched scream that can only come from a terribly frightened chimpanzee. The screeching woke the twins from their sleep and they quickly realized that driver ants were already in their beds as well as in the little box with Sadi-Ju. As they came running into our bedroom we wakened immediately and ran next door to the Marwiehs for help. It wasn't long before all the mission children surrounded our house with torches, beating the ground and turning the driver ants around to make them return to their own homes! Every night after that I worried that they would once again invade our bamboo house and get in the crib with Marion Sue. Later I learned that driver ants did indeed find their way into the crib of another missionary's baby. The parents found their baby eaten alive one morning by these vicious little creatures.

It wasn't long after that episode that Sadi-Ju was sleeping soundly in a cage right outside our bedroom when driver ants once again paid an unexpected visit. The little chimp had spent the evening with us in the house, eating at the dining-room table, and making her usual grimaces in imitation of some of our family. Earlier in the evening, Del had taken her for a ride on the motorbike, which she really enjoyed. When they finally put her to bed in her cage she was totally exhausted and must have gone into a deep sleep. Next morning when they took Sadi-Ju her breakfast of bananas, she was stretched out on top of her box – but nothing remained of our little chimpanzee but bones. The driver ants had completely devoured her.

We never found a way to insure that driver ants wouldn't return but Jack did locate their 'bug a bug' hill and poured gasoline down the hole. However, when he lit the match the explosion almost took him up in the air along with all the ants. We had fewer midnight visits from our little friends after that.

The pegboard walls in my bedroom allowed those tiny fireflies to flicker in and out. They were actually comforting to me during those dark nights in the midst of that jungle which held so many unknowns. Somehow I felt encompassed by the loving hand of God as I watched His tiny creatures light up the darkness with their miniature lanterns. It was like when He said to Abraham, 'Fear not, for I am with thee' (Gen. 26:24). Fireflies in my bedroom were just a reminder of that eternal truth.

12

'YOU'VE COME A LONG WAY, BABY!'

You would think that after 25 years of married bliss, this Yankee Officer and his Southern Belle would have a big impressive celebration. Well, we did. Sort of …

Actually, it was C.T. Studd who put the plan for the 25th in motion. Jack was reading the book, *Cricketer and Pioneer*. In this book, C.T. Studd tells how he begged his wife to come to Africa so they could spend their 25th wedding anniversary together. At that time Jack was still pastoring the church in Picayune, Mississippi, yet he said to me, 'We're going to celebrate our 25th wedding anniversary in Africa!' At the time his statement seemed like an impossible dream but it turned out to be reality.

Although it still seemed like a dream, here we were in a bamboo house in the middle of an African jungle. Our furniture from the States had not arrived, hammocks were strung across the screened-in porch and the front door that had not been hung was being used for a dining room table. Besides, how romantic can it be with four children and an old man (Bud Skelton) joining us for dinner?

We were able to put enough flowers in the hammocks to camouflage the little table for two I had managed to set up so that we had some privacy. Jack even put on his dark suit (suffering, I am sure, from the jungle heat) and we almost felt like we were back at the Broadwater Beach in Gulfport, Miss.! One problem we did have, however, was that the 'juice' I made from Christmas cherries (these red berries made great 'plum jelly') had fermented in the little kerosene refrigerator and tasted so much like wine that my preacher husband wouldn't drink it. Other than that, I had come a long way from a flirty teenage college girl in a nightclub on the Gulf Coast to a missionary on this remote mission station in Africa! Just like that ad says in the magazines, 'You've come a long way, Baby!'

13

DIRT, LEAVES ... AND COW MANURE

It didn't take me long to realize that our greatest enemy was not the diseases, the snakes or even the contaminated water. The thing I came to fear most was the 'country medicine'. This witchdoctor's brew of dirt, leaves and cow manure (or something similar) was used for almost anything. The first time I was made aware of this danger was when I was called to the village to see a little girl who had fallen into the fire.

The girl's name was Comfort and she had accidentally fallen in the fire two days before they came for me. The concerned people took me into the dark hut and showed me the girl, of about eight years old, lying on a bamboo mat. She was still wearing the same dress covered in ashes from the fire that she had fallen into.

As the room was so dark, and it was impossible to see the burns, I asked the people to bring her outside. Someone found a bamboo chair and they propped her up in it and I was able to see her charcoaled burned face in the sunlight. She was not only blackened by the burn but also by the 'country medicine' of dirt, leaves and cow manure that had been rubbed into her face. Infection had already begun to spread over her eyes and down her neck. As I took out my bottle of clean water and mixed it with soap, I said to the people, 'I am going to have to scrub all that medicine off her face. It is going to hurt. You will need to hold her.' They repeated this to little Comfort in her dialect as she did not understand English, but she replied, 'You do not need to hold me. I will not fight.'

True to her word, Comfort barely flinched as I scrubbed and scrubbed until all that dirt, leaves and cow manure was washed off. But after I put the Furacin ointment and clean dressing on her face it suddenly struck me like a bolt of lightning, 'I can't leave her here. As soon as I'm gone, they will put that country medicine right back on the burn.' So I turned to the people and said, 'May I take her back to the Mission with me to take care of this burn?' Surprisingly, they agreed.

For several months Comfort became a part of our family. Every day I gave her injections of penicillin, cleaned her swollen burned face and put on new dressings. Her eyes began to open and her face began to heal. Comfort's heart began to open as well. Every night when I put her to bed, I would sing to her, 'For God so loved the world He gave His only Son....' and Comfort would say, 'Sing it again,' and 'Sing it again.'

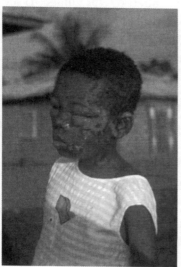

Doctors who have seen pictures of Comfort when she first came with her face burned and her eyes swollen shut from infection and later ones of her burned face completely healed, without even a scar, have said it is a miracle. Yes, it is a miracle she survived and a miracle that her face healed without a scar. But the greater miracle is that Comfort took Jesus into her heart before she went back to her village. But that enemy, the 'country medicine' seemed to rear its ugly head everywhere I went.

Comfort, after her face being burned in fire.

Babies were usually delivered outside huts because there was so much superstition. If the mother or baby died within the house the people believed that it would spoil the rice stored in the roof of the house. So I would

Comfort's face after God's miraculous healing

be called, usually at the last minute, to come and help pick the babies up out of the dirt outside their huts. There was one baby that I could not scrub clean. I took the little one home in the middle of the night and woke up Jack to help me. When the baby finally had all the dirt washed off I wrapped it in a blanket and laid it beside our daughter, Lisa in her bed. She was quite surprised the next morning to see this tiny bundle nestled next to her!

When I finally did persuade the wife of one of our pastor's to deliver their baby in the house, I was really careful that everything should be done in completely sterile conditions. And it was. So it was a shock and an unwelcome surprise when, a few days later, she came with the baby to tell me it would not feed. It only took one look to realize the baby had tetanus. I couldn't believe it. I had been so careful! What I didn't find out until later, however, was that the old grandmother had come from across the river with her 'country medicine' of dirt, leaves and cow manure and rubbed it into the baby's navel! We tried our best to save the baby, even taking it into Greenville to the hospital there in the hope they would have some way to treat the tetanus, but it was too late.

We never did see victory over that enemy. The belief in the healing power of the witchdoctors was too strong. Nevertheless, more and more people came to our little bamboo house for help.

14

HERE COMES THE BRIDE

A canopy of palm branches shielded us from the hot African sun. The morning had been overcast, but as midday approached the clouds rolled back and the bright sun appeared in the sky. We had prayed it wouldn't rain. We didn't want anything to dampen this very special day, the wedding day of our son, Vann and his fiancé, Christine Phileon. We knew there would be hundreds of people dressed in their finest clothes walking from their remote villages to witness the occasion. It was the first Christian wedding to take place in the forest of Sinoe County. The preparations for this day had been enormous!

Vann and Christy traveled from the United States all the way to Liberia so that Jack could perform the wedding ceremony. Vann had always said his dad was going to marry him and, when we could not leave the Mission to go back to the States, Vann and Christy decided to have their wedding in the middle of the jungle! Little did I realize when we agreed to do this what a jungle wedding would entail! First of all, we had no wedding dress. Christy wanted to make her own dress out of the 'country cloth'. Neither did we have bridesmaids' dresses, tuxedos for the groom and best man or dresses for the two little flower girls. So a trip to Greenville, fifty miles away, was necessary.

Christy selected beautiful colorful cloth and, with the help of a few 'sew-ers', as the male tailors are called, she made all the dresses and shirts that were needed to make this a 'proper' wedding! She and Vann had matching gowns, Donna (Bill's wife) and Lisa wore matching dresses as did little Marion Sue and her friend, Sophie Marwieh. Paul and Palmer, as ring bearers, wore matching shirts and carried the rings carefully on woven bamboo plates. Jack and Gus Marwieh both wore the traditional 'chief's robe' and looked very impressive as they performed the ceremony.

It was a bit distracting, however, when our pilot friend, Bud Heinzeg, from the nearby Leprosy Mission flew over the airstrip and dropped rolls of toilet paper from the plane! Other than that, the wedding was everything we could have asked. The multitudes of village people sang and danced and waited for the palm butter to be served. Traditionally we had to kill a cow and feed all these people. Vann tried to help by using the winch on the jeep to heist the cow up to allow the blood to drain but, in doing so, cut his ring finger.

As Christy wanted a fruit cake, which is traditional in her native Canada, we had to gather together all those special things that go into a fruit cake, things that just are not found in the bush. We began by having to 'candy' orange peel, lime peel and pineapple. Then we borrowed raisins, powdered sugar and even tiered cake tins from Martha Robinson, one of our missionary friends in Greenville. We also ended up 'borrowing' her oven and taking the batter into Greenville to bake. Our small butane oven was too risky for such a delicate work of culinary art. We even grated fresh coconut for the two white cakes that also graced the wedding reception table. I went into the forest myself to look for the perfect leaves to decorate the table. Del dipped them one by one into aluminum paint. You wouldn't believe what beautiful decorations they made around the cake and punch bowl! The punch was made from fresh lime juice which took one of our missions students the entire morning to squeeze. The top of the wedding cake (since we couldn't run to the store and buy a bride and groom or wedding bells) was drawn by Christy on cardboard, cut out by Jack, and then dipped in aluminum paint by Del. It was two hearts joined in the center by a cross, symbolizing being united in Christ.

Jack and some of his carpenters built a beautiful arbor covered by palm branches, about 100 feet long, right down the middle of the airstrip. At one end was a raised platform and, on the steps where the bride and groom would kneel and receive the benediction, was laid an animal skin rug of brown, black and white diamond-shaped design.

All of Nell and Jack's children present for Vann and Christy's Jungle Wedding.
L to R: Del, Bill, Vann, Christy, Donna, Lisa
L to R bottom row: Palmer, Marion Sue, Sophie Marwieh, Betty Marwieh, Paul

As the rays of the sun shone through the palm branches we remembered the promise God gave to Abraham: 'Jehovah Jireh', the Lord will provide. The Lord HAD provided! He had given us everything we needed for a memorable wedding for our son and his beautiful bride, even in the middle of the jungle. When as the mother of the groom, I watched the bridal procession walk down the aisle under the arbor of palm branches and counted one, two, three, four, five, six, seven children and two daughters-in-law, all under the African sky, there could only come forth a prayer of 'Thank you, Lord!'

Jack's family were not able to attend the wedding but somehow, because of the prominence of his family, I suppose, Vann and Christy's wedding in Liberia was given a two page spread in the Society section of the *San Jose Mercury Herald* newspaper!

Marriage in Liberia was still just a settlement of the bride price between the parents of the bride and groom, with no thought of being joined together by God. This Christian wedding attended by hundreds of tribal people was bigger news in the jungle than it could ever have been in *The San Jose Mercury*!

15

TRIED BY FIRE

'Fire! Fire!' the local children shouted. 'House on fire! House on fire!'

The mat house next to our bamboo house was indeed on fire but as we ran outside and looked back, the flames leapt over to consume ours as well. It was all over in minutes. One of the twins, Palmer, ran back into the burning house to rescue his favorite 'elephant' table, Jack tried desperately to save the china closet which held the precious plum jelly I had just made but he couldn't manage to get it out by himself. Lisa threw her typewriter out the window and some of the workers took the dining-room table from the house before the roof collapsed. The thought went through my mind then, as it was to do again years later when the rebels invaded Yekepa, 'I can't believe this is happening to me'.

We stood, stricken and silent, on the airfield as we watched the blazing fire and everything we owned go up in smoke. The tropical sun was hot. It was almost noon but no one could move. Little Marion Sue had run outside barefooted but one of the children quickly took off her own sandals and slipped them on Marion's feet. All the mission children knew my insistence that shoes should be worn to protect against the parasites that lurked in the African dirt. The village people came crying and wailing, 'The Mission is burning down.'

The people fully expected us to pack our bags and leave. Instead, we waited until the fire had died down and left a mass of smoldering ashes. Then, almost instinctively, Jack and I with the twins and Marion Sue turned and started walking down the airfield to the cement block house Jack was building for us at the end of the airstrip. Lisa followed slowly behind us. She loved that bamboo house so much she had refused to even go see the new building. When she caught up with us, choking back tears, Lisa said, 'Mother, remember what the Bible says, "Lay not up for yourselves treasures upon earth, where moth and rust doth corrupt, and where thieves break through and steal: But lay up for yourselves treasures in heaven, where neither moth nor rust doth corrupt, and where thieves do not break through nor steal: For where your treasure is, there will your heart be also"' (Matt. 6:19-20 NKJV).

I needed to hear that. I honestly had thought that by 'leaving' so much in the States, I had really sacrificed. I now realized I had not suffered materially at all. We had absolutely everything we needed. We still had 'treasures' on earth and every day, even in the jungle, we were accumulating more and more, so much more than any of the people around us.

It took me by surprise when, the next day, one of our pastors in training asked to see us. As Jack and I sat down with him, he said, 'My people have sent me to say, "Thank you." We asked, 'For what?' And he answered very quietly, 'Because you have taught us a great lesson. When your house burned down, and you lost everything you owned, you were not crying. You were smiling. You showed us that all those things you had did not mean as much to you as the Lord Jesus. You were trying to comfort us. We want to thank you for that.'

It was true. There was so much moaning and wailing as all the village people crowded around us that we had to reassure them that we would not leave them desolate. We would still be there with the medicines they needed, still have the mission school and the pastor's training school. We were there to stay. The fire did not burn our love for them or our love for Jesus and what He had called us to do.

Of course, that night we had nowhere to sleep. But before the darkness could envelop us with the threat of hopelessness, we heard the sound of a car coming in on the bumpy road. The missionaries from the leper colony some fifty miles away had come to 'carry' us back to their mission for the night. There they had food for us, clean clothes and toys for the children. As I tucked little Marion into bed, I suddenly remembered she didn't have her blanket with the silk edge but she quickly reassured me, 'When I get to be five, I won't need it any more.' That was true of a lot of the things we lost in that fire, we realized. 'We don't need them any more.' Only the Bible teaching notes I had so laboriously written over the years were hard to give up and thinking about them brought an ache to my heart. God must have known I needed to write them all over again just so I wouldn't forget all those incredible truths He had taught me. We learned a lot from that fire. And God had other purposes yet to be revealed.

Jack preached in one of the villages several hours' walk from the Mission the next Sunday. It was there that I had my eyes (and my heart) opened to see how generous and loving the Liberian people are. Lisa had lost her watch in the fire and one of the women in the choir noticed this. After the service she came over to Lisa and timidly took her own watch (something rare to see on a village woman with hardly more earthly possessions than the lappa on her back holding her tiny baby) and put it on Lisa's wrist. Another woman took me by the hand and led me to her thatched hut. There she climbed up into the 'attic' and brought down a beautiful silk nightgown. As she presented me with this treasure of hers, I was humbled – and ashamed – that I had had so much and held most of it tightly in my hand. It's just as the Bible says, true giving is not giving out of one's abundance but rather giving when you have very little to give.

I am certain God had many lessons to teach us from that fire. One became clear years later. As Jack kept the bricklayers working overtime to finish our cement block house, we stayed in a small bamboo hut on the airfield. A Southern Baptist missionary in Greenville found out about our plight and offered us a place to stay in what was then known as the closest thing to a 'resort' in Liberia, the mining community of Yekepa. As one of their missionaries was on furlough they had an empty house that we could use while our cement block house was being completed.

We had really never heard of Yekepa until then. As we drove over the miles and miles of dusty, bumpy dirt roads I wondered if it was worth it. Suddenly we hit beautiful paved roads! Suddenly it seemed there were LIGHTS everywhere and then real houses, paved streets, running water you could drink without boiling, five tennis courts all lit up at night, an Olympic size swimming pool, golf course, grocery store, movie theater and an International School! Surely this was Utopia rather than Yekepa!

It was in this incredible setting that, a few years later, God directed us to establish the first African Bible College. Right in the center of this amazing community, built to entice Europeans to come and work for the LAMCO Mining Company, that company was to GIVE us twenty acres of land for the college. We would never have discovered this jewel if there had been no fire.

What had we lost, then, in the fire? A bamboo house, furniture, clothes, books, medicines and study notes. Then there were the teaching materials, cameras, tape recorders, projectors and kitchen utensils. But all those things could be replaced. Had we really lost anything of worth? Or had we gained?

If it is true what the Bible says, that only those things that can stand the test of fire shall last, then there was nothing burned to the ground that day that was of any real and lasting value. And what we had gained will last forever. As a result of the fire we have seen souls come to Christ and be saved for eternity. We have received LOVE from the African people that cannot be taken away. We have had our FAITH increased as we experienced the marvelous grace of God in a time of trial. And we have set our HOPE more strongly than ever on our treasures in heaven and not on this earth.

So, FAITH, HOPE, LOVE abide. Fire cannot burn them. Waters cannot quench them. 'Yet indeed I also count all things loss for the excellence of the knowledge of Christ Jesus my Lord, for whom I have suffered the loss of all things, and count them as rubbish, that I may gain Christ' (Phil. 3:8 NKJV).

After receiving word of the fire, our oldest son wrote from the States and asked, 'God never makes a mistake ... does he?'

'No, my son,' we wrote back. 'God never makes a mistake!'

16

THE PIED PIPER OF MISSIONS

Harlow Willard, the pastor of the Rose Hill Presbyterian Church in Kirkland, Washington, once called Jack the Pied Piper of Missions. He said that if we were to land a plane in the parking lot of the church, Jack would have it full of people ready to fly off to the mission field. That could be true. He was always thinking of ways to get more people involved in missions.

The VACANGELIZE program did just that. Jack called it 'a new concept in missions' and it certainly was. Until the early 1970s there was very little being done in the way of short-term missions. VACANGELIZE was the perfect answer to getting more people out on the mission field.

The idea of combining vacation with evangelization had a tremendous appeal, especially among those who were tired of wasting their time and money on meaningless vacations that turned out to be the same year after year. Jack made it clear that the financing of this 'vacation' would not come out of the church's budget, but it would literally be a 'family vacation', paid for with the family's vacation funds.

When the idea was first presented at my home church, First Presbyterian Church in Jackson, Mississippi, the very first couple to respond were Frank and Catherine Hagaman, one of the most prominent and respected couples in the church. Then the Beales, Lois, Gilbert and all their teenaged children from Montgomery, Alabama wanted the experience of actually living in Africa and helping to spread the Gospel. James and

Katherine Yelverton of Magee, Mississippi used all their savings to participate in this exciting new venture and said later that it changed their lives. They are still some of the most ardent supporters of our work in Africa.

Jack had built a little house right on the beach in Baffu Bay, on the Liberian coast. It was a remote area only accessible by plane or canoe. We dropped the families off with a month's supply of groceries and a short-wave radio. From then on they were on their own! They were to teach the local pastors in that area, hold vacation Bible school for the children, and on the weekends they could use the dugout canoe for fishing or traveling up the river to a nearby village to preach in a church.

Month after month the people came. Dr Dale Boersma and his wife, Helen, brought their family and not only taught but also did medical work and even helped me in my clinic at ENI. Their eight-year-old son, Mark, was so impressed with the tremendous need for doctors in Africa that he later went to medical school and then back to Africa to work at the African Bible College Clinic in Malawi.

The VACANGELIZE program was a huge success in helping Jack to train the 100 pastors that had been left to Gus Marwieh by R. G. LeTourneau when he closed down his work at Baffu Bay. We probably would never have heard of Baffu Bay if it had not been for the fire that burned down our bamboo house.

One of the pastors in training at ENI Mission was a man by the name of William Kambleh. He and his wife, Mary, had lived at Baffu Bay when LeTourneau was trying to make it into a mission station with a hospital, huge church building, pastor's training facilities and even some fund-raising projects like rearing chickens and growing vegetables. For some reason they had to close down the mission and the little mission station became a ghost town. The monstrous cement block church was only partly finished and other buildings and equipment sat empty and deteriorated for lack of use.

But one day, after the fire, William came to us and said, 'Mother, you and Reverend have visited all the other villages where the pastors are from and have slept in their towns, but you have not slept in my town, Baffu Bay.' I replied, very defensively, 'William, how can we sleep in your town? We have nothing to carry with us. We have no way to take anything with us, no way to take water or food, or bedding or mosquito nets.' I will never forget the way William looked at me as he said quietly, 'Mother, we're human beings, too, you know.' Those words went straight to my heart. There was no excuse; we had to go. As we climbed into the little Cessna 180 I couldn't help but wonder how on earth I could take care of four children in a place I'd never seen.

The beach at Baffu Bay (Liberia) where Jack
built the first 'VACANGELIZE' House.

William didn't tell me that his wife, Mary, had worked with one of the American nurses when the LeTourneau Mission was in operation. He didn't tell me that she spoke perfect English (unusual for a woman in the interior of Liberia). He didn't tell me that Mary was a great cook and knew how to take care of 'white people'!

LeTourneau had left a long, beautiful airstrip and the little plane landed without any difficulty. As we waved goodbye to the pilot and walked along the water on a white sandy beach, under the shade of the tall coconut palm trees, I thought, 'This is the most beautiful place I have ever seen.' Mary ushered us into the empty church to a room complete with a double bed made up with sheets and blankets. There was even a pan of hot water for a bath. Then she brought us a delicious dinner of chicken with palm butter and rice, and fresh pineapple. When morning came Mary was there with hot coffee for us, Ovaltine for the children and fresh homemade doughnuts. I felt so ashamed for my lack of faith! I knew that God in His Providence had brought us here for a greater purpose than to 'sleep in William's town.' This place was like a Bethel for Jack. It was here that God gave him the perfect setting for the VACANGELIZE plan and it was here on this sandy beach under the Indian almond tree that God would reveal to him an even greater plan for the whole continent of Africa.

The Pied Piper of Missions was soon whistling his tune and many, many would follow and many, many lives would be changed – on both sides of that vast ocean.

17

'Go ye, swift messengers'

The little Cessna 180 was a great airplane. It was perfect for the short strips cut through thick forest. Our pilots, Bud Heinzeg and George Call, missionaries with the Canadian Assemblies, were the best. Nevertheless, Jack was always concerned about losing that one engine and landing on top of those tall trees! And so it was that as the VACANGELIZE program began to formulate, I said to him one day while we were still on furlough in the States, 'Honey, we need our own airplane!'

Jack agreed. He had recognized the value of the Cessna 'push-pull 337' with its two engines and its ability to keep flying even if one failed. We mentioned this to our friends, Pam and Wilson Benton, who had

Pilot Bud Heinzeg and Jack beside the Chinchen's new 'push-pull' plane ... *The Spirit of Cleveland.*

followed us faithfully during our time in Liberia. Without any hesitation whatsoever they said, 'The church in Cleveland can get that airplane for you.' Wilson was pastoring the First Presbyterian Church of Cleveland, MS, and the congregation was growing not only in numbers, but spiritually as well. He felt they had the faith to 'attempt great things for God.' And they did.

The Church rallied behind the idea and soon the entire town of Cleveland became involved in buying this airplane for the missionaries in Africa. It was an exciting step of faith in action. God truly went into motion and, on a beautiful spring day in 1973, Bud Heinzeg flew *The Spirit of Cleveland* into that city with the words from Isaiah 18:2 'GO YE, SWIFT MESSENGERS' emblazoned boldly on her side. The Town Hall bell was rung and the Mayor himself was present as we christened *The Spirit of Cleveland* with water from the Mississippi River.

As Jack and I stood in front of the plane with Lisa, Marion Sue and the twins along with the Mayor of Cleveland, Wilson Benton and Bud Heinzeg to have our picture taken for the newspapers, the thought went through my mind, 'Is anything too hard for the Lord?' (Gen. 18:14). No, nothing is too difficult for Him. It is only our lack of faith that holds Him back. Now our Vacangelizers could mount up with wings of eagles in *The Spirit of Cleveland* and we could fly safely over the dense jungle in the Sinoe rainforests of Liberia. Once again God had been glorified by moving hearts to supply 'all our needs,' just as He promised He would.

George Call, the Chinchen's pilot, Missionary with Liberian Assembly Mission standing by the "Spirit of Cleveland" ready to take them into the remote areas of the Jungles of Liberia. He was later killed when he flew into a mountain in northern Liberia.

18

LIGHTNING STRIKES

Lightning struck, and in one flash of light two of our little mission girls were gone. Four of the girls attending the ENI Mission school had walked out to the cassava farm to cut cassava. Two of these little girls slipped off their rubber sandals and tossed them into the metal pans they carried on their heads. As they looked up at the darkening sky, and fearing the rain, all four made a dash for the nearest tree. Just as they reached the huge lone tree, and sought cover under its towering branches, a bolt of lightning struck it, knocking all four girls to the ground. Two of them never got up again.

Jack was in the classroom teaching the pastors when the two other girls burst in screaming, 'Come quick! Come quick! Lightning Hit! Lightning Hit!' Jack jumped into his jeep with as many of the men as could climb inside and roared down the dirt road to the farm. As he ran up the hill to the cassava patch, he could see under the lone tree the two little girls lying with beautiful, peaceful looks on their faces, but dead. These two girls were the most committed Christians on the mission. Why? Why?

It took a while before we were able to answer that question. 'Unless a grain of wheat falls into the ground and dies, it remains alone; but if it dies, it produces much grain' (John 12:24 NKJV). Those two little girls died physically that others might live eternally. Many of the students at ENI Mission, including three of our own children, gave their hearts to Christ as a result of that tragedy.

But God still wasn't finished with us. Sixteen days later, almost to the hour, lightning struck again. The vicious crack jolted me as I was in my study teaching Marion Sue. She immediately said, 'Let's pray!' As the noise of the thunder bolt faded, screams came from all across the mission station. Children in almost every building had been hit by the seven bolts of lightning that came crashing down like seven fingers of God.

Marcus Solo, one of our students, was on the floor of a classroom unable to move from the waist down. Again there was that odor of burned flesh. As we were picking him up, we heard the boys yelling in the dormitory, 'Emerson was hit and is on the ground.' Then the girls from the girls' dormitory were screaming, 'One of the girls has been struck and is not able to speak or move.' We went down the airfield to check the students at the other end of the campus and found that another boy had been struck. When we returned to our house we saw that not only had our chimpanzee, DeeDe's chain been melted in half, but a bolt had crashed into the house, knocking down plaster both outside and inside. Sitting inside, stunned and burned, was a student who had been knocked down while standing on our porch. We were all very grateful that no one was killed and we were able to treat those suffering from burns and shock.

The students were terrified. Some of them even left the mission station vowing never to come back. The village people, led by the Chief, came the next day en masse seeking prayer. They claimed the Mission was witched and, when they found the person doing the witching, they intended to make him drink the deadly sassa wood. I don't think they ever did determine who the 'witch' was, but Jack pored over his Bible trying to find answers to these strange happenings. He did.

We had been having a lot of discipline problems with some of the students. Nothing we did seemed to change their rebellious behavior. When Jack preached the following day in our Chapel service he used Scripture verses out of Job, 36:32 (NKJV) 'He covers his hands with lightning, and commands it to strike,' and Job 37:13 (NKJV) 'He causes it to come, whether for correction, or for His land, or for mercy.' The title of his message was, 'Lightning, God's Rod of Correction.'

The need for discipline was over. ENI Mission now could once more be a light in that dark jungle. Forty students received Christ after the lightning struck and a renewed awe of God prevailed. As the song *How Great Thou Art* says:

I see the stars; I hear the rolling thunder,
Thy power throughout the universe displayed.
Then sings my soul, my Savior, God, to Thee
How great thou art.
(Stuart Hine)

19

'HONEY, WE NEED A HOSPITAL'

The four ammunition boxes filled with medicines put together for me by Dr John Seimens in Port Angeles were soon depleted. Dr Seimens (who had delivered the twins) was concerned that we should have the medicines we needed to take care of our family as we lived in the remote jungle. But it was not long before all the village people and mission students as well were at the door of the bamboo house seeking medical help. I had no choice but to share what we had.

Fortunately, Dr Gus Hemwall and his wife, Helen, flew into our little mission station and I soon realized we had friends! As we walked together along the jungle trails to visit the sick in the nearby villages I shared with Gus how I was treating different tropical diseases. I was amazed that he agreed with everything I was doing! I soon found out that the Tropical Medical Manual I was using was written by his partner, Dr Adolph, missionary to China! It was not surprising that I was doing everything 'right'!

After he went back to Chicago, Dr Hemwall arranged to have MAP (Medical Assistance Program) send us boxes and boxes of medical supplies. And the people kept coming. The new cement block house Jack built after the bamboo house burned down had a special room for my 'clinic' but it wasn't enough. I said to Jack, 'Honey, we need a hospital!' He agreed, and when we were next in the States and we were asked by the Missions Committee at the Main Street Presbyterian Church in Columbus, MS, what was one of our greatest needs, Jack told them of the hospital unit that was being offered by the United States government and the State of New York.

Complete 'insides' of hospitals had been prepared in case of atomic attack. These units were being offered without charge to missions and groups overseas if they would cover the shipping charges. The cost to ship one to Liberia was $5,000, a lot of money in 1973! The contents of these packages was unbelievable: complete burn ward supplies, obstetric supplies, surgical instruments of every conceivable type, medicines, bandages, blankets, cots, refrigerators, generators and pumps. There was everything but the building, and that was already available at the Mission. Providentially, a missionary had built a large mud block building with tile floors, windows with screens, and individual rooms – a perfect hospital. She had intended using it for an orphanage but became too ill to remain on the field and turned the building over to us. All we needed was the $5,000 to ship the 'hospital' to Liberia.

The Missions Committee listened to our story and then asked, 'Why don't you tell the Church about this tonight at the evening service?' But Jack replied, 'We never make any financial appeals.' When the committee insisted we tell about the opportunity, Jack said to me, 'You tell them.' So I did.

Nothing earth-shaking really happened, but on the way out the door, one old man said to us, 'I'd like you to stop by my farm on your way home. I keep bees and I'd like to give you a jar of honey.' As we had the children with us, and it was a long drive back to Jackson, I said, 'I don't know if we have time. We need to get the children to bed. They have school tomorrow.' But he was pretty insistent and we agreed to stop and get that jar of honey.

We went to old Mr Yeleverton's home and waited for him to bring the honey. When he came back he had his checkbook along with the jar. He sat down at his wooden desk cluttered with papers and wrote out a check for the $5,000 we needed to transport the hospital to Liberia! The children were happy to get the jar of honey, I was happy to get my hospital and we were all overjoyed to see once again that God moves in mysterious ways His wonders to perform.

Honey, I need a hospital … and a jar of honey!

Nell holding a new born baby in front of her clinic before the hospital was built.

20

LEPROSY IN THE LIMELIGHT

Leprosy has always been prevalent in the tropics. That dread disease was feared even as far back as Old Testament times. Now that I knew we would have a 'real' hospital, I was certain there would be a lot of leprosy patients to treat and I needed to learn more about it. The Leprosy Training School at Carville, Louisiana is one of the best known and well staffed such institution in the United States, and probably anywhere in the world. Dr Paul Brand and his wife are both authorities on this debilitating disease. Jack encouraged me to go there for some training. He said he would take care of the children and the house so that Leta Simpson and I could take advantage of this opportunity to learn how to diagnose and treat leprosy. Leta and her husband, Grady Simpson, were going to Liberia as missionaries under CNEC to work with the Gbaizon tribe and she, too, would be doing some medical work. So we went together. I confess I was somewhat apprehensive that I might 'catch' leprosy at the training school, but those fears were soon dispelled when I became more knowledgeable of the disease.

We benefited greatly from the teaching of the Brands and the other doctors who taught us. Not only did we learn about leprosy, but other tropical diseases too. It was well worth the time and effort and the children and Jack survived amazingly well! When I arrived back home and went into our bedroom, there on the bed was a brand new camera. It was a 'graduation' present from my husband!

That is the kind of encouragement that has kept me stepping into difficult and impossible situations – a husband who has wanted me to be used of God to my highest potential, and a God who is willing to use even the most unlikely people to accomplish His purposes. The people in the jungles of Liberia needed a hospital, a 'doctor' and medicine and there was no one else to bring it to them. So He allowed me to have that joy and that privilege.

I really didn't expect to go it alone. We asked and asked for a doctor to come and help us but it never happened. Several times we had doctors visit to see 'if they liked it', but they never did. All my training proved to be worth it if only for one little boy, Solo. Solo was a friend of Paul and Palmer. He played soccer with them; he played games in our house with them and he was one of their best friends.

The day he came to me and said, 'Mother, I have a sore on my leg that won't get well,' my heart fell down (as the Liberians would say). When I looked at the sore all those pictures of leprosy I had seen at the Leprosy Training School came rushing back to my mind. I knew immediately that this was no ordinary bruise on his leg; this was something that could destroy this young boy's life. Solo had leprosy! Just the word sent pangs of fear through my body. But I also had hope.

As we needed a firm diagnosis, I asked Jack to drive us to the Leper Colony at the nearby Mission. (Nearby meaning only an hour or two drive, depending on the conditions of the roads.) There, I knew, was LaVerne Emerson, a nurse trained especially to take care of the leprosy patients at their mission station. She was able to do the lab work that determined, yes, it was leprosy. 'But,' she said hopefully, 'fortunately, you have caught it in its early stages! I can give you the medicine and you can take him back and treat him yourself!' Good News? I wasn't so sure. How could I take Solo back to our mission station and put him in the dormitory with the other children? How could I have him playing with my twins … in my house … every day? But I knew I had no other choice. I also knew that the risk of transmitting leprosy when it is under treatment is infinitesimal. So we took Solo home. God healed him of that dread disease. But more than that, God healed him of the dreadful consequences of a life separated from Himself. Solo became a Christian, once again demonstrating to us that God's plan is greater than we can understand. We need only to be obedient to whatever He asks us to do.

Part V

Why us? –
by Faith in God

Life in the Jungle

Ready for their plane trip to Monrovia.

Welcome to ENI MISSION

Nell and Jack in front of their bamboo mat house built for them by the tribal people eager to welcome their first white missionaries.

Happy to be in their new home with new friends:
L to R: Mother George; Gus and Othella Marwieh; Marion; Nell; Lisa;
L to R bottom row: Isaac, George, and Floyd Marwieh; Paul and Palmer

Airstrip in front of our bamboo house.

Unloading boxes for hospital at ENI Mission.

Welcomed by the people of Liberia.

Jack's 92 year-old grandfather (John D. Crummey, founder of FMC) being carried in a hammock by people from the nearby town of Plantibalibo.

Grandpa Crummey with the twins and chimpanzee, Sadi ju.

Lisa, Nell, Grandpa Crummey; and Marion engulfed with Liberian children (Paul and Palmer in the midst).

Del and Robert carrying their
water from the creek.

Driver ants marching to invade the
Chinchen's bamboo house.

ENI student, Marie Wah,
ready to boil the Chinchen's
water for 20 minutes.

Paul, Palmer, Lisa, and Marion holding their pets.

Chimp getting a motor bike ride with Del.

Lisa receives the gift of her goat, STAR, from the village people after a church service.

Del giving Sadi-Ju her bath.

Marion Sue being carried 'Liberian Style' by ENI Student, Marie Wah.

Jack reading a bed-time story to Chimp and the twins.

'Overflow' when Jack preached at a village church service. Looking on, Marion Sue; Palmer; Geoge Marwieh, Paul.

Lisa and Nell crossing the river with an umbrella to protect them... not from rain., but from the aggressive Green Mamba snakes that jump from the trees!

Jack and Del cross the river on a home made raft.

Crossing the river in a dug-out canoe carved from a tree log.

All that's left after the Chinchen's bamboo house burned down.

21

Under an Indian almond tree

Elijah lay down in despair under a juniper tree. Jack caught a vision for the continent of Africa under an Indian almond tree.

The little VACANGELIZE house we built was on a sandy hill overlooking a bay of the Atlantic Ocean in Baffu Bay, Liberia. At the bottom of the hill was an Indian almond tree whose branches spread widely and whose large green leaves gave welcome shade from the hot African sun. It was under this tree that Jack sat one day in a reclining lawn chair with his pad and pen and listened to God as He outlined a bold plan for spreading the Gospel across the vast continent.

Jack and I had talked and prayed a lot about our concern for the young high school graduates in Liberia, especially for the Christians. When we first went in 1970 only five per cent of the population was receiving high school diplomas, but that number was rapidly increasing. The University of Liberia, though offering good quality education, was only able to accommodate a small proportion of these graduates. There were but a few smaller graduate schools in the entire country. Thus there was a great need for a university-level institution with a Christian emphasis and a four year degree granting program. A Bible college was certainly the answer, but how could that be accomplished? God had a plan. Without a doubt He revealed his plan to Jack that day under the Indian almond tree.

Soon after we flew back to ENI Mission God confirmed that plan by a strange providence. We were sitting in our living room after the children were in bed and reading by Kerosene lanterns. I was reading a book called *Expendable, The Story of the Prairie Bible Institute* by Philip Keller. It was about the founding of Prairie Bible Institute in Three Hills, Alberta, Canada. To us, it was confirmation that we were on the right track, that God was leading us into a ministry that was bigger than we were. Once again we were thrown back on that promise in Proverbs 4:12: 'As thy goest, thy way shall be opened up, step by step, before thee' (ancient Hebrew version). We knew we had to venture out in faith.

22

THE SHANGRI-LA

Yekepa was carved out of the jungle, cradled in its arms, even though the imprint of civilization had hardened its contours. The aura of the jungle was there. We sensed it especially at night when the jungle sounds penetrated the darkness: the drums beat in the distance, the call of the crickets and the serenade of the birds brought their songs in the night to lift our spirits after a long and exhausting day.

I had become so captivated by the jungle in Sinoe County that I didn't think I could have borne to be totally deprived of the deep joy that the jungle gave me. It is indeed beautiful. My eyes loved to feast upon its beauty – so rich, so lush. But the sounds made my heart beat faster and sent a smile across my face. It's the excitement, perhaps, that one becomes addicted to, the living dangerously that so captivates.

And so it was that the first African Bible College was hewn out of the core of this Shangri-La. The towering Nimba Mountains filled with some of the richest iron ore in the world stood like a protecting giant behind the College and the City of Lights, as Yekepa was known, surrounded the campus. The campus was soon to be a bustling little city in itself, with palm trees lining the road and pathways, and students moving up and down those paths as they rushed to classes or meals at the dining hall. The story of this emerging college is an amazing series of God's providences.

23

'MOTHER, DID YOU HEAR YOUR BIRD SING?'

I didn't want to leave ENI Mission. I loved the jungle – the thick bush, the tall trees and the birds that sang. Yet I knew that God was calling us to something even more meaningful for his kingdom. Still, I wanted to be absolutely certain that we were in His way and that none of this was our idea. I spent many hours on my knees, weeping and pleading for some positive sign from Him.

The day we arrived in Yekepa to 'see' if God was leading us to establish the Bible College there, I still did not have peace about leaving our work at ENI Mission. Lisa, Paul, Palmer and Marion were with us and we were staying at the little Lutheran Guest House next to the beautiful Swedish built Lutheran Church. The morning after we arrived Jack went down to the Administrative Office of LAMCO to see about an appointment with the General Manager. I stayed in our bedroom on my knees praying and weeping and earnestly seeking God's perfect will. Finally, in desperation, I decided to 'put out a fleece.' 'Lord,' I prayed, 'if I hear my bird sing I will take it as your will that we come here.'

'My bird' became my friend and comforter during a bout of illness that was probably lassa fever. I was so sick I could hardly lift my head from the pillow. My eyes were almost swollen shut; my gums were so swollen and bleeding that I could barely swallow liquids as my throat was swollen and sore. But one day I heard this bird singing in the low bush near my window. It had the most unusual song! Actually, it sounded like the whistle of a human being. It sang two distinct tunes, one cheerful and lilting and the other very low and mournful. But the melody so lifted my spirits that, when I felt better, I asked one of the people what they called the bird. 'Oh,' he said, 'that's the too-a-loo bird! He's a beautiful bird with feathers every color in the rainbow!' And when I mentioned his unusual song, he answered, 'Oh, the people say, he's happy because his father killed an elephant, but he's sad because his mother died!' That explained his 'two tunes'!

I knew, even as I put out my fleece, that the possibility of hearing my bird sing in Yekepa was extremely unlikely. The too-a-loo bird lives in the low bush in the rain forests. Yekepa had very little low bush and all the forest had been cut down to make room for the community. I felt pretty safe! Suddenly, from the next room, Lisa called out, 'Mother, did you hear your bird sing?' I listened ... and, sure enough, there was that familiar whistle – happy, yet sad. That was just how I felt. I was happy that the Lord was calling us to a new and exciting work, yet sad to be leaving the place I had come to love so much.

The next few hours were to confirm without any doubt that the answer to my fleece was revealed as God's providential circumstances began to unfold. In just one day He opened door after door to provide the property, the perfect location and the assurance that He not only wanted an African Bible College, but that He wanted it in Yekepa!

Jack had gone early in the morning to try to find out where we should begin the search for property. We weren't sure if the land belonged to the government, the local tribe or the company itself. The previous evening Jack went into the local market and asked the Lebanese merchant that very question. His answer was another indication that God was arranging these providences to accomplish His will. 'It's interesting you should ask that question. The company has just recently decided to open up the city of Yekepa to outsiders. The man you want to see is Charlie Roberts.'

With this information in hand, Jack went to the Administration building in hope of being able to make an appointment with the Vice President, Mr Charlie Roberts. It didn't take long for him to be ushered into the office of the Vice-President of this huge corporation. When the secretary said, 'Mr Roberts can see you now,' Jack realized that something important was about to happen and he didn't want me to miss out. So, he told the secretary that he would be right back and rushed out the door to the guest house nearby. He came rushing in with the news that the Vice-President was willing to see us and that I should hurry and come with him!

We were both surprised when we walked through the door of the office to find, firstly, that Mr Charlie Roberts was a distinguished elderly Liberian (this was primarily a Swedish company and all the other executives were Swedish), and secondly, there was an open Bible on his desk! As Jack presented his desire to build a Bible College in Yekepa, Mr Roberts said excitedly, 'That's just what we need here! A Bible College! Do you have a car? Would you like to drive around and find the property you would like and then come back and we will go see the engineer and determine if it is available.'

And that's what we did. We drove around Yekepa and, when we had found what we felt would make a good location for the college, we went back to the Vice President's office and he took us to see the General Manager of LAMCO. He and the engineers along with the rest of us in the office ended up on the floor looking at maps of the area. In just a matter of hours the LAMCO Corporation had agreed to GIVE us the land we needed to build the first African Bible College.

Jack later went back to thank Charlie Roberts and was surprised when Mr Roberts said, 'You need to see the President and tell him what you are going to do.' Jack answered, (thinking he meant the President of LAMCO), 'But we've already met with the President.' Charlie Roberts said emphatically, 'I meant the Present of Liberia!' Jack answered somewhat hesitantly, 'I don't know the President...' With this response, Mr Roberts said, 'I will give you a letter to introduce you to President Tolbert.'

That was why when we left Yekepa we drove straight to Monrovia to see the President instead of heading back to Sinoe County! We had two weeks in Monrovia before our appointment with President Tolbert, two weeks to put together the entire plans for a Bible college. Lisa was there with a small borrowed typewriter and she helped to compile an attractive book on the Proposed African Bible College, with pictures of all the amenities in LAMCO, Yekepa. There was also time for me to have a beautiful purple satin 'lappa' suit with elaborate gold stitching made and for Jack to have a tailor-made wool 'total involvement' (short sleeved) suit fitted for this auspicious occasion. President Tolbert was a Baptist minister and noted for his receptiveness to Christians. Nevertheless, we were humbled when he invited us to go behind his desk to show him the 'book' we had prepared. He graciously insisted that we call him 'Brother Tolbert.'

No doubt about it, when Lisa said, 'Mother, did you hear your bird sing?' she was reminding me that God is Sovereign. The too-a-loo bird can sing even when there's no low bush and God can move hearts and mountains to make room for a Bible college in the midst of a mining community if that is what He chooses to do.

Presenting a picture of the proposed African Bible
College to President Tolbert, of Liberia.

24

MISSION ACCOMPLISHED

The Pensacola Institute in Pensacola, Florida had been the venue for a family ritual ever since we moved south and Jack became pastor of the First Presbyterian Church in Picayune, Mississippi. Every year during the month of August we eagerly attended 'THE' Institute. Not only did we have an opportunity to fellowship with old friends, but we were privileged to hear some great Bible scholars as they preached and taught every day at the McIllwain Presbyterian Church. All our children looked forward to this family vacation as they too would see old friends, friendships that still last today. They also enjoyed all the planned activities for really young people as well as teenagers. Even after we became missionaries and could only go to Pensacola every few years, it was still a highlight for our family.

So, it was natural that our first stop upon returning to the United States for furlough each year would be the Pensacola Institute. Jack shared with the pastor, Don Dunkerly, his vision for a Bible college in Liberia. Don, who also had a heart for Africa, called his mission committee together and gave us the opportunity to share the plan we felt God had given us for a four-year, degree-granting Bible College. Jack even laid out the twenty-one buildings he felt were needed and the cost to build each one. The total amount was somewhat overwhelming to these conservative men but one of the members of the committee, a plumber, spoke up. 'Sonny,' he said to Jack, 'If you were to break these figures down and divide them by three,

I think churches could handle that. It's going to take you three years to build this college so you really don't need all that money at once.'

It was as though someone had turned on a light. All of a sudden this huge undertaking took on reality. What a great plan! Churches could take an individual building and pay for it over a three year span! In order to get the ball rolling that little old man with big faith put a check for $5,000 in Jack's hand to go toward the first building on the African Bible College campus. So it was, that as Jack and I spoke in church after church, the buildings for the college became popular items.

A demonstration of our motto 'Faith in Action – God in Motion' is the Macon Gymnasium. Jim Baird, who was then pastor of the First Presbyterian Church in Macon, Georgia, asked us at short notice to fly up for the weekend to share our testimony with the college group in the church. Don Patterson, who was the keynote speaker, would also be flying with us in a private plane. As it turned out, one of the pilots was a Reformed Seminary student and, though a good pilot, he had not done much recent flying. So, when the gas tank became empty and the engine sputtered, it took him a little while to remember he could switch tanks to the one with the fuel! During a rainstorm in mid-air, with the little plane bouncing about in dead silence, every one of us wanted to make sure we were 'right with God' – just in case we didn't make it to the ground alive!

Jack and I both love sharing what God has done in our lives with college kids. They have their whole lives in front of them and how great it is when they turn their lives over to God for His use! We were really excited as we told them the story of the Bible College and how God had worked to underwrite all the buildings for the campus except two, a men's dormitory and the gym. Jack said that we really didn't need the gym right away and, if we could find someone to take the boy's dorm, we would be ready to start building. After the class was over, a tall young man came up to us and said very seriously, 'I'm a basketball player and I've been training for the Olympics in a university in Florida. I think that gym is important. You've been talking about "Faith in action – God in motion", well, I have just ten dollars in my wallet, but I want to give you that as a down pay- ment for the gym!'

We arrived back at the Mission House at Reformed Semi- nary in Jackson and had no sooner walked in the door when the phone rang. 'Hey, I hear those buildings are going like hot cakes!' a voice said. 'What do you have left?' It was Jack Ross, pastor of the Faith Presbyterian Church in Brookhaven, Mis- sissippi. 'We have the boy's dorm and the gymnasium left to be underwritten,' Jack answered him. Jack Ross said, 'We'll take the dormitory!' and hung up the phone!

The next day, Jim Baird called and said that the missions committee had agreed to underwrite the men's dormitory. Jack said, 'I'm sorry, Jim, but the dormitory is already taken. But let me tell you a story.' So he told him about the young man putting his faith into action and giving his last ten dollars for the gym. It didn't take Jim long to see God's hand in this. He went back to his committee and they agreed to take on the gym and to let the college group give the extra $5,000 it would cost to build! There is now a Macon Gymnasium not only in Liberia, but in Malawi and Uganda African Bible Colleges' campuses as well. When it was time to return to Liberia, I was reminded of the verse from Psalms: 'He that goeth forth and weepeth, bearing precious seed, shall doubtless come again with rejoicing, bringing his sheaves with him' (Ps. 126:6).

Our mission was accomplished. A new mission organization, African Bible Colleges, Inc., was chartered in the state of Mis- sissippi by our good friend, Bob Cannada. A Board of Directors was set up with Buck Mosal as Vice-President (later we added Jack Ross and then Bill Herrington, Wilson Benton, Jim Baird, Don Blackburn, Tom Kay, Bob Massengill, Ed Williford, our son, Paul, Jim Moore and Mark Linsz – an auspicious list of Christian leaders). Tax exempt status was granted. Commitments had been made by various churches and individuals to underwrite all 21 buildings. And our son, Del, and his wife Becky agreed to oversee the construction.

Jack's vision under the Indian almond tree was beginning to blossom.

Our dream for educated, dedicated young people who could turn Africa right side up, was about to be fulfilled. But the testing was not over yet. There would still be uncertain, trying days ahead.

The artist's rendition of the African Bible College taken from drawings of Missionary Tech Team who designed the campus.

25

ORANGE BLOSSOMS AT BIOLA

'BIOLA ATTRACTS FAMILY OF NINE' the headlines of the Biola University *Chimes* publication read. Underneath the picture of this unique family was the statement: 'Members of the Chinchen family believe the family that studies together stays together.' Over the past 25 years this has proven to be true, as eight of these children have served together with African Bible Colleges in Africa. Actually, the headline should have read: 'BIOLA ATTRACTS FAMILY OF TEN,' for it was not long before Marion Chinchen met Stephen Spencer at Biola and they were married before she and Steve graduated. Biola is a private evangelical Christian university based in Los Angeles.

The article read: 'The children of Jack and Nell Chinchen have established a unique tradition. Unlike most family traditions, the pattern did not evolve over time, nor has it been passed from one generation to another yet. It is not a seasonal celebration observed by children and grandchildren. There are nine Chinchen family members presently pursuing graduate and undergraduate degrees at Biola University.'

Del and Becky went there first. Del was working on his doctorate in missiology and Becky was completing her Bachelor's Degree in Christian Education while Vann sought his Masters of Divinity at Talbot. Paul, a Communications/ Intercultural Studies Major, later went to Reformed Theological Seminary and then completed his doctorate at Stellenbosch in South Africa. Lisa was also studying

Christian Education while her husband, Steve Rief, joined her brother at Talbot. Paul's twin, Palmer, was working toward his Intercultural Studies degree and he later received his doctorate from Trinity Seminary. His wife Veronica was majoring in English while Paul's wife Laura was studying to become a speech therapist. Marion, as a freshman, had yet to meet her future husband, Steve Spencer, who received his Master's Degree from Talbot and later a Ph.D. in Education from Stellenbosch University.

Later on, some of their children would also attend Biola but the frosting on the cake, which wasn't mentioned in that article, is that Reverend Jack Chinchen was given an honorary doctor of Laws degree (LLD) from Biola. I don't think it was because he had so many of his progeny attending that College, but rather that Biola recognized the value of Christian higher education in Africa which 'Doctor' John W. Chinchen was propagating. Interestingly, at the same ceremony where he was awarded his Honorary Doctorate, Paul Chang was honored in the same way. Paul Chang, who was with CNEC, was the messenger God used to call us to Liberia! Another missionary, Don Richardson, author of *Peace Child*, was also on the platform. It was quite an exciting and impressive array of God's servants.

In the article Del related the amazing providence of God in sending him and Becky to Liberia to help build the first African Bible College. As God had given the vision for the College, and had supplied the finances to build the college, as well as the land and the building, there still remained the question, 'Who would handle all that construction as well as land for the college?' Del had graduated from LeTourneau College with a degree in Missionary Technology and with that degree came some very practical training in building with cement block. He was the perfect person to oversee the construction of the campus! As Del tells the story in the article, 'Only days before receiving the request, Del and his wife, Becky, mailed a letter to his parents announcing their decision to pursue missions. They asked if the couple needed help in Africa.'

Del said the apparent coincidence of the two letters crossing in the mail was an answer to prayer. He said he felt that he and Becky were on the right track, and began preparing for their new roles in missions at Biola. 'Biola University is known for its strong evangelical stand in Missions as well as its broad liberal arts offerings.'

Picture of the Chinchen Children at Biola Bible College:
L to R top row: Christy, Vann (Nell and Jack) Del, Becky, Laura
L to R bottom row: Marion (not married to Steve Spencer yet, who also went to Biola); Lisa, Steve Rief; Palmer; Veronica; Paul

The article elaborated on the fact that all of the nine Chinchens expressed an interest in returning to Africa to further their parents' vision for Bible colleges there. 'No matter what the Chinchens decide to do, it seems their family tradition stands to impact lives far beyond their immediate family. Biola's goal to "equip Christian leaders to make an impact on the world" may be realized through their lives.'

Nevertheless, the orange blossoms had to bloom at Biola before this unique legacy could be left for the next generation. God used Biola Bible College to put together the teams that would make it possible for African Bible Colleges to impact Africa, and to impact the world.

26

FLIES ON THE SNICKERDOODLES

Our arrival back in Liberia in August 1977 was uneventful. Jack was asked to preach at the International Church located on the ELWA (Sudan Interior Mission) compound for a few weeks before we left for Yekepa to begin building the Bible College. The miracle had been accomplished: all twenty-one buildings had been underwritten, government approval had been given, LAMCO had allocated land adjacent to their administrative building and across the street from their International School. God had done the impossible.

We were in daily contact over short-wave radio with Del and Becky who had gone ahead of us to begin the construction work. Every day there were new and exciting reports of how rapidly things were moving ahead. The Company did everything possible to assist us in getting the land prepared and connecting us with water and electricity. God was at work even in the hearts of those who did not know Him.

But we were missing out! We were 'stuck' in Monrovia! I was beginning to get restless for the bush. I missed the closeness of the people, the sounds of the jungle and the beating of the drums from the nearby village. It was difficult to stay confined in a fine house on a mission station in a 'city'. I guess God knew my heart was hungry for my people for He brought Africa to my door ... on the INSIDE!

It was a rainy afternoon. Thinking the children might like some cookies, I went to the kitchen and found in an old cookbook the recipe for snickerdoodles. I was stirring up the batter when one of those terrible biting flies began chasing me around. The yard boy was outside washing windows. I said, 'David, there's a biting fly in here!' A few minutes later, I turned around and saw him lift the spatula from the hook over the stove. 'What are you doing?' I asked. 'I'm going to get that fly-o,' said David, as he swatted at the fly vigorously with a spatula! When I tried to explain that the spatula was not a fly swatter, I don't think he really understood.

A few minutes later he was inside again with a nice clean bucket which he filled with hot water. I thought he must be going to use it to wash windows, but when I questioned him, he said, 'No. I'm going to take a bath and it's too cold to use regular water.' It was a surprise to me that, as he only came for a few hours a day, he took his bath here.

It didn't strike me as too strange, though, when Marion Sue and one of her friends came in with a monkey. They call this kind, 'Softly, softly, catch monkey' and they're quite easy to tame. About the same time, Paul and Palmer came running through the kitchen with their camera in an old sugar bag. It was pouring down rain, but, 'Never mind, yah, we're going to take a picture of a soccer team, the team that Goo-Foo plays in.' Goo Foo (Liberian English for 'good food') happens to be the cook for the house where we are staying. He does make good bread, but the last time he cooked rice we almost broke our teeth on the sand he had failed to rinse out! When Goo Foo plays soccer, I cook.

I was taking the second batch of snickerdoodles out the oven when someone knocked on the door. 'Tie-Dye lady from Sierra Leone,' a voice sang out loudly. I almost burned my hand trying to decide what to do with the hot cookie sheet full of cookies! I found them a resting place and rushed to the door. 'I'm Christina,' the woman smiled, and I could see right away this was no ordinary tie-dye lady! She was dressed like a model out of a magazine. All of a sudden I really felt grimy and tried to wipe the flour off the front of my dress ... but just added more.

Christina came in with her little girl, her two suitcases full of tie-dye material and, in perfect English, (I knew from that she was truly from Sierra Leone and not Liberia!) asked if she could show me her cloth. I was so fascinated by the tricky way she tied her head-tie, the two lovely stones around her neck, the perfect match of her lappa and sandals, and the expensive gold earrings with the map of Africa inside, that I totally forgot the snickerdoodles! I forgot about them, that is, until a terrible burning smell came drifting into the room.

After a hasty rescue of what was left of the snickerdoodles, I sat down to watch Christina unfold yards and yards of beautiful tie-dye cloth. What gorgeous colors! Some even had designs. There was a map of Africa and a chicken on one piece (I'm not quite sure why that particular combination). On that dreary, rainy afternoon the bright colors spread out all over the living room was as though a rainbow from the African sky had come right inside the house!

I quickly calculated how many pieces of cloth I could buy and still have money left for groceries, rationalizing that these would make really good presents for people. After the proper amount of bargaining back and forth (in Liberia, you never pay the first price asked) we settled on a price. It was in Christina's favor, but somehow I didn't mind that. She said she had a 'fixed price' and I believed her.

Her daughter began to fold up the pieces of cloth neatly, packing them into the suitcase while Christina made notations in her notebook of the sale. I looked at her (such regal beauty!) and asked, 'Are you a Christian?' 'I am a Moslem,' she replied. 'Oh,' I said, 'that's the wrong way. There's only ONE WAY to get to God and that is through Jesus Christ.' She sat patiently as I explained the way of salvation, but her eyes had a distant look and I knew she wasn't listening. Finally, as she was leaving, I said, 'Try to find a Christian mission in Sierra Leone, Christina,' as I shut the door. Well, I tried, I thought, but somehow didn't find much satisfaction in that.

The burning smell still lingered in the kitchen. It was time to get dinner on and the table ready. What had happened to the afternoon? I suppose my thoughts were still on Christina for, when I served the cornbread, I noticed that I must have baked it with ANTS on top because there they were – hundreds of cooked ants on top of the cornbread.

But this was Africa. The 'small small' things like flies on the snickerdoodles, ants in the cornbread, monkeys in the living room and Moslems on the doorstep were just parts of everyday life as we waited impatiently to begin the operation of the first African Bible College.

It was during this brief stay in Monrovia at the ELWA Mission Station, however, that the urgency of the call God had given us became even more vivid. Ritualistic killings were becoming more and more frequent. As a body washed up on the beach had parts missing that had been offered as sacrifice, we knew more than ever the need for Christianity to reach deeper and deeper into the hearts of the people. It was during this time that President Tolbert called for a Day of Prayer and Fasting that these merciless killings would stop. A town meeting was called and the scripture verse from 2 Chronicles 7:14 was proclaimed to an audience of hundreds of concerned people. 'If my people who are called by my name will humble themselves and pray and seek my face, and turn from their wicked ways, then I will hear from heaven, and will forgive their sin and will heal their land' (NKJV). This was President Tolbert's plea. We knew without a doubt that African Bible College could be used of God to help to bring healing to that great nation.

27

GABRIEL ISN'T ALWAYS AN ANGEL

Bible College by Radio was part of the vision given by God under the Indian almond tree in Baffu Bay. Jack had the great idea that a Bible teaching program including interaction with our students would appeal to the Africans; they enjoy dialogue so much. And it did. ELWA Radio Station in Monrovia accepted our pilot programs and in no time we were on the air!

Jack originally intended doing all the programs himself. They were thirty minutes each and went out five days a week. But he soon realized that was a huge undertaking and asked if I would do the teaching (which included writing the lessons) two days a week. Bible College by Radio was broadcast over the forty-nine meter band in 1977, before the College was built.

Over the past thirty years we have attempted to teach every book in the Bible and these lessons are still being taught. Along with the lessons taught over the radio, each student who requests it receives a free booklet which includes questions concerning the

Nell, broadcasting Bible College by Radio over ELWA with student, Gonwo Dahn.

lesson that the student may answer and return to the College for grading. As ELWA expanded to include the sixty and seventy-five

meter bands the lessons were aired in the surrounding countries
of Sierra Leone, Ghana, Nigeria and even French-speaking Cote
d'Ivoire and mail came in by the thousands! Many African Bible
College students earned their scholarship by grading and mailing
the booklets. And Jack and I stayed up nights to write the script
and study the Bible to prepare the lessons on time.

Before the College was built and we had our own recording
studio, we had to travel by train each month to Monrovia in order
to record enough lessons to last through the next weeks. While we
were away, Del and Becky took care of Paul, Palmer and Marion
for us. We seemed always to be under pressure to meet a deadline!

Jack and I were grateful
for the LAMCO trains
that enabled us to travel
so easily to the 'big city'. It
was a three hour journey
to Buchannan and then
a long taxi ride into
Monrovia. Later we found
we could put our car on the
train and drive the hour
and a half from Buchannan
to Monrovia. These train
trips always proved to be

Nell and Jack waiting for LAMCO iron ore
train to take us to Monrovia to broadcast our
'Bible College by Radio' programs over ELWA.
(Sudan Interior Mission)

interesting and usually an opportunity would open up to share the
Gospel. Lisa taught at a Calvary Chapel Christian School when
she first graduated from Biola and Chuck Smith's son, John, gave
her hundreds of copies of the Gospel of John, beautifully presented
in magazine form and very appealing looking. We always took
stacks of these to pass out to everyone on the train! We never
had anyone refuse to take one.

On one of these trips we took the twins and Marion Sue
with us. We had a cooler box with cold drinks as the train was
not air-conditioned and was often very hot and humid. On
this particular occasion a prisoner was brought on the train,

handcuffed, and surrounded by police officers and soldiers. They were seated not far from where we were and I could easily hear the prisoner begging for something to drink. The soldiers and police mocked him as they drank their bottles of beer and refused to give him anything. He kept begging for even a drink of water and, when they refused, he began to swear and use very violent language. After a while, I could take it no longer and I grabbed a cold Coca-Cola out of the cooler box and went to where he and his 'friends' were sitting. As I had heard the soldiers calling him 'Gabriel', I said, 'Gabriel, I have small children on this train and they should not hear that kind of language. If you promise me you won't talk like that any more, I will give you this Coca-Cola.' He meekly nodded his head and I handed him the cold drink. Gabriel was completely silent the remainder of the trip.

I knew they were taking Gabriel to Bella Yella, a prison from which no one returns, and I wanted to give him a Bible. But the only one I had was my own pocket New Testament, a beautiful leather-bound volume that I cherished and really didn't want to give away. I gave in to the prompting of the Holy Spirit and went over to the distraught prisoner. 'Gabriel,' I said, 'I want to give you this Bible but you must promise me you will read it.' Once again he nodded his head and with his handcuffed hands took that little New Testament and put it in his shirt pocket. As we left the train and were putting our bags into the back of a taxi, Gabriel came over to us and tapped that Bible with his bound hands, and said, 'Thank you for the Bible. I promise to take good care of it and to read it every day.' With those words he was led away to an unknown destiny. But I know without a doubt that God put us on that train together to fulfill His purpose for Gabriel, who was certainly no angel. Perhaps like Gabriel in Scripture who had a special message for Daniel, and Zacharias and Mary, he had a special message for me – God's Word is to be given away, not kept only for ourselves.

And that's exactly why God has blessed the ministry of Bible College by Radio. The daily reaching out of God's Word into multitudes of lives for these thirty years has enriched the Kingdom of God more than we will ever know. His protection over those lessons was shown during the war in Liberia. The former President, Samuel K. Doe, was very angry because Charles Taylor had announced over the ELWA radio station that he was now the President of the country of Liberia. In order to retaliate, Samuel K. Doe, prepared a truck called the 'Russian Organ' and fired rockets on the ELWA compound. Many facilities were destroyed, including the radio station where all our Bible College by Radio programs were stored. Providentially, however, we had begun broadcasting these same programs over Transworld Radio in Swaziland. Even Satan in all his fury could not destroy God's Word. Bible lessons that had taken Jack and me years to write and record were still safe and secure all the way across Africa nestled in the little Kingdom of Swaziland. They were waiting to be revived and broadcast, not only over Transworld Radio, but later over our own Radio ABC-Lilongwe, Radio ABC-Mzuzu and Radio ABC-Uganda ... and, fifteen years later, over ELWA-Monrovia, Liberia once again!

Gabriel, blow your horn with the message that God's Word is alive in Africa!

28

YOU SHALL PUT YOUR EYE ON YOUR TEACHER

Liberians have an expression for every type of situation. One of their favorites is, 'I want to put my eye on you!'

The morning after our return to Liberia following our furlough in 1981, Jack and I were having our devotions when suddenly there was a knock on the door. We were staying in the little cottage at ELWA called 'Shorehaven', overlooking the beautiful beach and Atlantic Ocean. We were spending more time than usual in prayer for we had a real need as we had failed to recruit the professors we needed for the College for the next school year. African Bible College was growing and as each year passed, another class was added. Qualified college professors who wanted to teach in Africa were just nowhere to be found. We had been beseeching God fervently to supply this desperate need. Hadn't He said, 'I will supply all your needs'?

The knock on the door startled us; we weren't expecting anyone that early in the morning. When I opened the door, I didn't recognize a familiar face. The man said, 'I'm Don Linsz. My wife, Barbara and I were wondering if you would all like to have dinner with us tonight.' We said we would be delighted. As he left, I turned to Jack and said, 'Listen to what I was reading in my Bible when he came to the door.' I read from Isaiah 30:20b: 'Yet shall not thy teachers be removed into a corner any more, but thine eyes shall see thy teachers' (NKJV). 'You don't suppose this could be our teacher, do you?' I asked.

Don and Barbara Linsz had served as missionaries in Ethiopia for several years but, as Don had complications from hepatitis, it was necessary for them to return to the States for a time. Then because of the political problems in Ethiopia, they were unable to go back there and had come to Liberia to work in the counseling department at ELWA. It was there that they became interested in the African Bible College students who were working at ELWA during their vacation. They were excited over what they saw in these students and were eager to meet us.

That day we found that we had a lot in common. Their two older children, Mark and Nancy, were close in age to Paul and Palmer. Both Barbara and Don had a deep love for the African that created a bond between us as we shared our experiences. Don, like Jack, had been a pastor, which is not as common as you would think among missionaries. We told them about our concern for more professors for the start of the new school year in August and asked them to make it a matter of prayer.

A few weeks later the Linszes were on vacation and staying in one of the houses on the African Bible College campus. Jack and I both wanted to go and ask them if they would like to come and teach at the College. But we knew that might be running ahead of God. So we prayed, 'Lord, if you want the Linszes here, let them ask us.' We had found from past experiences that this is one sure way to discover God's will even though it is not the EASY way!

That evening we took Don and Barbara up to the Mountain View Restaurant for dinner. We told them again about the need for teachers but we were careful not to say what was burning in our hearts, 'We need you! HELP!' The next morning Jack was up on a ladder trying to repair part of the roof on our house when Don yelled up to him, 'I'd like to talk to you over in your office.' When Jack came in the house to tell me, we knew God had answered our prayers. And so it was. Don shared with Jack how he and Barbara had not been able to sleep all night, how they felt God was calling them to teach at African Bible College and could we use them? Could we!

Truly, we had put our eye on our teachers! No longer were our teachers hiding in a corner. ELWA was willing to help with staffing, recognizing that African Bible College was meeting a need for their expanding work in Liberia. Thus Don and Barbara became vital parts of what God was doing through African Bible College in raising up Christian leaders for West Africa.

29

COUP D'ÉTAT

The little short-wave radio was perched on the edge of the dining room table as close to my ear as possible. I was trying desperately to concentrate on addressing the piles of invitations in front of me and, at the same time, listen to voices saying things utterly impossible to understand or believe. Almost as quickly as I addressed one envelope, however, what I heard on the radio made me throw it in the wastebasket at my feet. The dignitary I was inviting to the dedication of the chapel at the African Bible College had just been tied to a pole on the beach in Monrovia and randomly shot at by drunken soldiers until they killed him. One by one those invitations landed in the wastebasket as I realized that there would be no dedication. There had been a coup d'état.

April 7, 1980 marked the end of an era. Liberia had been the only Christian democracy outside America for over 150 years. Settled by freed American slaves sent by the Mississippi Colonization Society in 1847, there had never been a major war. Tribal conflicts, and even attempts to dislodge the settlers, yes, but by and large it was a peaceful nation. The Constitution had been patterned after that of the United States. There was a Senate and House of Representatives. The National Anthem clearly rang out, 'Glorious land of Liberty, by God's Command.' Liberia considered herself to be a Christian nation. There was never a thought or a fear that one day this would all come to an end.

President Tolbert was an Americo-Liberian, the title given to those who were descendants of freed slaves. For over 150 years they were the 'ruling class'. Americo-Liberians were well educated, held all the public offices, and considered themselves superior to the native Liberians, the tribal people. Other nations, including the United States, were beginning to say that the time had come for the tribal people to have the opportunity to govern Liberia.

The Minister of Education of Liberia congratulates Nell and Jack on African Bible College being accredited as a University.

No one knows how the coup actually came about. Soldiers simply walked into the Presidential Mansion in Monrovia and killed President Tolbert. The events of that night are too sordid to repeat, and too heartbreaking because when we met with President Tolbert to ask permission to be allowed to begin a Bible college, he insisted we call him 'Brother Tolbert'. He was a Christian, a Baptist preacher, and had done nothing to deserve such a violent death.

On that Saturday morning my heart was pained with the news on the short-wave radio. It took a while before the reality of it all began to break and then my heart was gripped with fear. Our twins were in the city where this was taking place! Where were they? Were they safe?

The American International School they attended in Monrovia was filled with children from the very families that were being targeted for execution. Even though the school was primarily for the children of the American Embassy families, it was also open to Liberians who were able to afford the high tuition costs. As we were given special rates it was possible for many missionaries to send their children there. Paul and Palmer had asked to go there instead of a boarding school in Ivory Coast. Now they were caught in the midst of a coup d'état.

We discovered later that the school barely skipped a beat. Classes went on 'as usual' while men were hung on poles and humiliated before being shot and killed by drunken soldiers. The twins began to realize that many of these leading citizens were the fathers and uncles of their classmates. Although fear hung heavily in the air, our sons had no way of escaping the city. All the roads were blocked.

Palmer had been visiting friends at the Voice of America station some 15 miles out of the city and was anxious to get back to the Lutheran Mission Hostel where they were living at the time. Paul and his friend Chris Clark decided to 'borrow' Chris' dad's car and drive out to get Palmer. On the way they were stopped by a very drunken soldier who put his AK-47 through the window and said, 'Give me your car!' Both Paul and Chris had been in Liberia long enough to realize that Liberians like to bluff. So, boldly, they refused. As the soldier kept insisting, they finally said, 'We will give you five dollars but not the car.' The soldier agreed.

The Liberian army was soon to become a major force in ruling the country. For months, even years, people were threatened and harassed by the military who seemed to be everywhere. Checkpoints with guards, police and soldiers were everywhere and they attempted to be as intimidating as possible. All we had to do when passing through the numerous checkpoints was to say the magic words, 'Bible College by Radio.' The guards would recognize our voices and wave us through! Even the soldiers were listening to our program over ELWA.

The day the military convoy came to the African Bible College campus in Yekepa we held our breath. We had no idea what the 'new government' would do with a Bible college. I can remember Del and Becky's baby, Joanna standing at the door of their house with her diapers hanging down, watching the army jeeps filled with soldiers carrying machine guns driving past the house to the dining hall. Del was still doing construction on the campus and was in shorts and a working shirt. Someone said to him, 'Del, you had better go put on some good clothes, these men are serious!'

As we gathered the students and faculty together in the dining hall, we had no idea what the outcome would be. Close the school? Turn it over to the government? Evacuate the missionaries? The Commander took charge and began his speech. We were to continue just as we were, he said. Nothing would be changed. This turned out to be absolutely true. In fact, it was through the new government's Accreditation Committee and Minister of Education that African Bible College became a fully accredited university. Interestingly, the man who spoke that day had attended a mission school in Sinoe County.

There were untold atrocities committed during the days after the coup in 1980 but not once did any of the disturbances touch the African Bible College. I am reminded of the verse, 'A thousand shall fall at your side, and ten thousand at your right hand but it shall not come near thee' (Ps. 91:7 NKJV).

30

HAM RADIO – A LINK TO THE WORLD

The Bible College in Yekepa was finally in full swing. The buildings were completed; the students were in the classrooms and the professors in place. Don and Barbara along with Bart and Ruth Bliss had been seconded to us by ELWA. With other qualified teachers they were beginning to train young people, of whom it would later be asked, 'What makes African Bible College students different?'

There were, however, a few things missing. One by one our children were beginning to 'fly the coop'. Lisa was married and living in La Mirada, California; the twins were attending Biola Bible College. Even Marion Sue was going away to boarding school in Ivory Coast. In those days before cell phones and e-mails, I felt cut off.

It was our old friend, Ed Ingles, who came up with a solution. 'Nell,' he said, 'if someone on your campus will get their Ham radio license, I will send the antenna and radio, and will even make phone patches for you here in the States so you can talk to whomever you like.' A great idea! The only problem was that no one really was motivated to learn all those algebraic formulae and Morse Code in order to qualify for a Ham license. Finally, I told Jack, 'Let me do it!' At the time we had a student from Sierra Leone who had been in the Signal Corps and he spent hours with me showing me how to use the Morse Code transmitter until, eventually, I could send and receive at fifteen words a minute – the speed required to pass the Ham Operator's test.

After that, every Saturday night we would contact Ed Ingles on the Ham radio and he would phone patch us to Lisa and Steve's house where Paul and Palmer would be waiting to 'check in'! Later, Marion was there as well. It was through that little Ham radio that we met future husbands and wives, gave counsel and in general kept close tabs on all those distant offspring. 'EL8J to W5GOU' became a familiar sound over the airwaves. That little Ham radio became a lifeline, a link to the outside world. Feelings of desolation and isolation can become acute in such a remote situation but that towering steel beacon became a source of great comfort, not only to me but to the other missionaries as well. For years, we would say, 'Over ...' whenever we talked on a telephone! In Malawi my call sign was 7Q7NC but it was EL8J that brought JOY to my heart on those Saturday nights!

Ham Radio License granted!

31

UNDER THE GUN

'Rebels in Yekepa?' Impossible! Jack had said very confidently that the rebels would NEVER invade Yekepa and he was usually right about those kinds of things. Old navy experience, perhaps? His reasoning for this was very sensible. The Nimba mountains towering over the little community of Yekepa were filled with some of the richest iron ore in the world. The mining corporation located in this remote city was the greatest financial resource for the country of Liberia. The rebel leader, Charles Taylor, knew this well. His mother came from the Gio, the very tribe that inhabited this territory. The rebel soldiers would NEVER enter Yekepa!

So when the rebels came closer and closer to the town, in the spring of 1991, we did not run away. We felt very secure until word filtered through to us that two missionaries only ten miles away had been ambushed and killed. Tom Jackson and his wife had been missionaries with the Inland Church denomination for decades. Out of their little mission school deep in the heart of the jungles had come some of the strongest Christians in the country. They had brought to the first class of African Bible College their most outstanding student, Amos Miamen. Afterwards they brought many other such dedicated Christian leaders to receive further training at our college. We knew them well and so did all the Mano/Gio people.

No one really knew exactly what happened but, as we pieced together the stories, it seems that President Doe's soldiers came to the mission station where the Jacksons lived and took them at gun-point to their own vehicle to be used as decoys in getting through the rebel-held territory. The rebel soldiers ambushed the car; shots were fired, and the Jacksons were killed. Their bodies were never found. When Charles Taylor heard of the tragedy, he declared a day of mourning for these faithful missionaries. He also called for a cease-fire and offered fervent apologies for the accident.

This incident triggered the U.S. Embassy in Monrovia to contact me (as warden for that area) on my Ham radio and demand that there be an immediate evacuation of all Americans. We were forced to close the Bible College. Jack was very reluctant to do this and he offered the opportunity to any of the career missionaries to stay if they did not want to leave. Bob and Carolyn Branch were adamant that they would not evacuate. So, the Branches and Jack and I stayed to protect the empty campus. Jack was still certain that the rebels would never invade Yekepa.

Palmer and his wife, Veronica, who was pregnant with their first child, drove our new station wagon with the convoy going to Monrovia. It was scary. There were lots of soldiers and numerous checkpoints along the way. In fact, when they arrived in Monrovia, they radioed back on the short-wave radio that their car was the LAST one to be allowed through. The danger of another ambush was imminent. They were supposed to take the next plane out to the States, but Palmer said on the radio to his dad, 'Veronica and I will not leave the country until Mom is out. I will try to find a plane and send for her.'

The next Sunday, Carolyn Branch and I were teaching Sunday School classes at the Mt. Nimba Baptist Church when Jack burst into my classroom and said, 'Hurry and get packed! The Colonel is coming into the Grassfield airport and Palmer has made arrangements with the pilot to take you and Carolyn back to Monrovia.' I didn't want to leave the Bible College, neither did Carolyn, but I knew it wasn't safe for Palmer and Veronica to stay in Liberia any longer and I wanted them to go home while they could.

I had one concern, how were we going to pay the pilot? I knew that the mercenaries were charging one thousand U.S. dollars for a one-way trip to Monrovia and I didn't have a thousand dollars. But then I remembered my two gold coins locked safely away in a drawer in my bedroom – another of God's amazing provisions. We had been in a mission conference in a small Louisiana town where we stayed in the home of a newly-married Cajun couple. This was soon after the 1980 coup d'état. They asked us one evening, 'When the coup happened in Liberia, what was the most frightening thing to you?' That was not a hard question to answer. We had no American dollars.

Without American dollars there was no way to get out of the country. Credit cards would not work; checks would not work, only cash. This young couple said to us, 'We collect gold coins. We want to give you two gold coins but you must promise never to use them unless there is a coup and you need to evacuate.' I had kept that promise and the two gold coins (worth over 750 dollars apiece) had remained securely locked away in my dresser drawer for ten years. I needed them now. But, as I was leaving Jack behind, I asked him, 'Do you want the gold coins, or should I take them?' He said, 'No, I don't need them. I don't plan to leave Yekepa.'

As we drove up to the airfield at Grassfield I was surprised to see barrels lined up on the airstrip. How could a plane land? There were also soldiers with AK-47s surrounding the entire airfield. They looked ominous. But as I walked around, shook each of their hands and told them I would pray for them, their faces changed. They were just as scared as I was. There was the roar of a plane and then all the barrels were quickly rolled out of the way and the pilot set the plane down on the grassy field. My heart was thumping as I watched the Colonel step off the plane and walk away. The Israeli mercenary pilot told Carolyn and me to get in quickly as he had to leave. I held those two gold coins tightly in my hand as I said, 'I don't know how I'm going to pay you but I have these two gold coins …' The pilot looked me straight in the eye and said, 'Don't worry. The Colonel has already taken care of it.'

The two weeks we spent in Monrovia were filled with the tension of impending doom. I didn't like it. I was afraid of a siege where we would be stranded without water, without food. To me, it seemed safer to be in Yekepa where the borders of Guinea and Ivory Coast were just a jump away. Every day we would tune in our short-wave radios and get a report on conditions at the College. On Easter Sunday Jack arrived on the plane from Abidjan. He, too, had been forced to evacuate. An entire caravan of over twenty vehicles drove across the border to Guinea and then through Ivory Coast. BBC reporters met the caravan in Man, Cote d'Ivoire, and gave a live interview over the radio about the Mining Company of Yekepa, Liberia, fleeing the rebel army.

Godwin Ofari-Attah, one of our students from Ghana, had stayed behind to guard the campus. Every day we were on the short-wave radio with him and every day he would respond, 'The rebels have not come into Yekepa. Everything is fine at the Bible College.' And every day I said to Jack, 'Let's go back. I feel safer in Yekepa than I do here in Monrovia.'

After almost two weeks of waiting for the invasion that didn't come, we decided to go back home. We had left two vehicles in Abidjan – the Peugeot and the old yellow mini van. We asked the Mid Baptist missionary, Brian Dickinson, if he would like to come with us and drive the van back to Yekepa. As Brian's wife and children had already left for the States, he agreed to come. We would have to fly from Monrovia to Abidjan and then drive over 500 miles to the border of Guinea and Liberia because the Ivory Coast border to Liberia had been closed.

A short-term Mid Baptist young man drove us to the airport. As I handed him all my Liberian dollars, we said to him, 'Why don't you come with us? It's not safe here in Monrovia.' He declined, saying that someone needed to stay at the mission station. As it turned out, he allowed some of the Mano/Gio people to take refuge at the mission and when Samuel K. Doe's soldiers discovered them, they burned down the station, killed the young missionary and threw his body on the steps of the U.S. Embassy.

We made it safely to Guinea using the paper from the mining company with its many stamps (officials in West Africa like stamped documents, the more stamps and the more documents the better) to clear the many checkpoints. As we reached Yekepa and drove into the Bible College campus we were enveloped with a sense of well-being and peace. And when I climbed into my own bed that night I said a prayer of thanksgiving. 'I'm home.'

The next morning we called some of the directors of the mine, Carney Johnson and Roosevelt Jones, who had also returned. I asked if they would like to have dinner with us and Jack and Carney even planned to play tennis later that afternoon. I drove down to the grocery store to pick up some meat for dinner and then I was going across town to 'P' market. Marion had asked me to buy David (her one year old) a little suit from the tailor there. Suddenly I was startled to see women running with pans on their heads, filled to overflowing with all their possessions. So, I stopped the car and asked, 'Where are y'all going?' One woman answered breathlessly, 'Haven't you heard? The rebels are in Yekepa!'

I turned the car around and drove as fast as I could back to the campus. Seeing Jack walking toward the library, I yelled out the window. 'Hurry! We have to leave! The rebels are in Yekepa!' Even then I could hear the sound of guns and rockets blasting in the distance. But Jack wasn't impressed; he was still certain they would never invade. 'That's just the soldiers shooting at trees!' he replied.

BOOM! BOOM! The noise was getting closer. I ran in the house and started throwing things into a suitcase. Jack said, 'I'll call the company and see what they say.' He talked to Carney and Roosevelt and both of them said they had no word that the rebels were in Yekepa.

I kept hearing guns blasting and they sounded like they were coming from my backyard. My hands were shaking as I threw things into my suitcase. Jack still refused to take my warnings seriously, but I knew it was time to go. Finally, he said, 'All right. Fix me some lunch and we'll see what happens.' As I put the tuna fish salad on the table I could only pour myself a glass of milk. My stomach was in knots; I knew I couldn't eat. Just as Jack sat down at the table, a huge BOOM exploded behind our dining room window. It didn't take us long to pile everyone we could into our old Peugeot and head for the Guinea border! As we left the house, I turned to Jack and said, 'You forgot to lock the door.' He just looked at me. I couldn't believe this was the end.

We drove to the top of the hill and stopped by Carney's house. He and Roosevelt were sitting in two bamboo chairs with a small table and the telephone between them. They were waiting for the call to tell them that the rebels were indeed in Yekepa and it was time to evacuate. We said, 'We will meet you across the border in Guinea.' And there on the top of the hill, we watched as the city fell without a fight.

Once again God had delivered us. But I almost felt like Lot's wife as He had to drag me out by the hand. I didn't want to leave Yekepa. I didn't want to leave my home that would surely 'last forever.'

32

THERE IS A RIVER

There is a river – the Yah River – that runs directly behind the Bible College in Liberia. In Psalm 46:4 we read: 'There is a river whose streams shall make glad the city of God, the holy place of the tabernacle of the Most High' (NKJV).

During the war the river provided much-needed water to our students and missionaries. It also carried a very dangerous insect which causes a disease called *onchocerca volvulus* or river blindness. While Del was building the Bible College, he was infected by one of these flies and consequently developed that horrible affliction: horrible, because it literally CAN cause blindness, and horrible because even the treatment is debilitating. Fortunately, he was able to have it diagnosed early enough to receive treatment and, in God's providence, a new treatment had just been discovered which made it possible to prevent the blindness that usually accompanies the disease. He is still under treatment.

Nevertheless, there is a river ... which makes glad the people of our God. We came very close to using that river for a hydroelectric system. Stuart Irby, from my hometown of Jackson, Mississippi had a great concern for Liberia and donated money for a feasibility study. Someone from Stanford University even came out to Yekepa to look into the possibility, but it was just about that time that the rebel invasion began and the study was put on hold.

I suppose now the only significance that river has is that it runs behind the African Bible College and it could very well have been the deciding factor that encouraged Del, Jack, Becky and me to make the decision to rebuild the College in Yekepa.

In January 2005, the four of us traveled from Monrovia to the College to try to determine if it would be possible to begin again. The usual four-hour trip took eight hours. There were some twenty-two United Nations check-points, all fortified with barbed wire and tanks and soldiers with AK-47s. The road was filled with pot holes and mud; without Kokee Kotee's fourwheel-drive vehicle, we would never have made it.

The only place open where we could stay was the Catholic Mission. Carol High School was still operating and the Mission gave us two small rooms in the back of their compound. But it was the next morning, when we went to the Bible College campus, that we realized how hopeless the situation looked. The buildings were so covered with jungle that we could not even find our houses. We had boys go in front of us with cutlasses to clear a path. As we pushed our way through the brush and out into the clearing, there was the Yah River, roaring through its banks, over rocks and ridges. We stood there looking at the rushing river when someone said, 'We could use the river to make electricity.'

Hope for the restoration of the College was being born in us. Instead of discouragement, there was a sense of excitement, of anticipation. God was ready to begin again. Jack was waiting for word that a mining company would come back in and reopen the mine, but now both he and Del said, 'Let's go for it, mine or no mine'!

That must be what God was waiting to hear. The day after we returned to Monrovia we were told that there would be a town meeting for Americans at the U.S. Embassy. At the meeting it was announced that Mittel Steel (the largest steel company in the world) was bidding for the opportunity to reopen the Nimba Mine in Yekepa. If that were true, then we would not have to worry about electricity as the mining company would furnish all we would need!

But there is a river that flows with memories of multitudes of students and missionaries who lived alongside that river and learned and taught God's Word, who played and laughed and lived lives that honored their Creator. There is a river that still makes glad the people of our God, the Yah River behind the African Bible College in Yekepa, Liberia.

Part VI

Where do we stretch forth? – by Faith in Action

33

THE WARM HEART OF AFRICA

As Jack and I sat together on the couch in the little living room of the Reformed Seminary Mission House in Jackson discussing this new mission organization, we were trying to come up with just the right name. We had already decided we liked the title African Bible College, but one of us (we are not sure which one) said, 'If this college is successful in training up Christian leaders, it should not be the ONLY one in Africa! We should put an 's' on the end and make the name of the organization African Bible Colleges.

And so it was, as we saw the impact our graduates were making on West Africa, we knew it was time to think about a second college. We are not certain how God communicated to Jack 'Malawi', but soon providential circumstances pointed clearly to this little country across the African continent.

The 'Land of Livingston' was first explored by David Livingston and at the time was called Nyasaland. A 400 mile long lake spans the length of this little country harboring some of the most beautiful fish in the world. Snuggled between Zambia, Tanzania, and Mozambique, open to Christianity, enjoying a stable government, surrounded by other English-speaking nations, this small country was the perfect location for a second African Bible College.

Our son, Paul, who was attending Biola University, wanted to go with us on our first 'exploration' trip. We had to go to Malawi the same way we traveled to Yekepa – by faith. We had no idea what obstacles we would meet but we set out remembering Proverbs 4:12: 'As thou goest, thy way shall be opened up, step by step, before thee' (ancient Hebrew version). And it was, indeed, a step at a time.

Our return from that first trip found us totally discouraged. We recognized immediately that there would be a lot of red tape with the government, with the church and with the educational system. Jack and I both thought that it looked like a mountain we weren't sure we wanted to try to climb! However, when we wrote Paul, who had returned to college, about our doubts, his reply brought us up short. 'Mom and Dad,' he wrote, 'where's your faith?'

God also spoke to us out of His Word. We were preparing to bring a report on our trip to the African Bible College faculty in Liberia and we had a lot of pictures to show and some stories to tell. Just before we left for the meeting Jack said to me: 'Do you have a verse to share?' I picked up my Bible and turned to Isaiah 54:2: 'Enlarge the place of thy tent, and let them stretch forth the curtains of thine habitations; spare not, lengthen thy cords and strengthen thy stakes.' I didn't know until later the significance of that verse and its most unusual history.

Several years before we went to Malawi, I had written beside this verse in my Bible, 'Second ABC'. It was quite a surprise to me when I became aware that this was the verse that began the whole missionary movement! In his book, *Promised-land Living,* J. O. Sanders wrote this:

> Let us recapture William Carey's vision. In his famous Nottingham sermon that sparked the modern missionary movement, he said, 'Thou shalt see greater things than these. Enlarge the place of thy tent! Lengthen thy cords! Strengthen thy stakes! Expect great things from God, attempt great things for God! Dare a bolder programme! Dwell in an ampler world! Launch out into the deep! The voice rang through him. The vision was blinding. Have you seen the vision, heard the voice? Will you pay the price?

This was just another confirmation that we must keep moving on … marching across the continent … putting faith in action and watching God in motion. Malawi here we come!

God always has His man. In Liberia it was Senator Harrison Grigsby. Later, in Uganda, John Mpyisy was mightily used of God to open doors that otherwise would have remained closed. Dr Fletcher Banda in Malawi was the Chairman of the Board of the prestigious Kamuzu Academy, often called the 'Eton of Africa'. This unique, private school was founded and operated under the auspices of the President of Malawi, Kamuzu Banda. Patterned after elite British schools, students were carefully selected and faculty all imported from England. The first exception to this was when an African Bible College graduate was given the position of lecturer in mathematics. It was because Fletcher Banda was highly respected by the President of Malawi that the way was cleared for African Bible College to be registered as a new mission organization despite a recent moratorium ruling against any new mission organizations being allowed in the country. Not only did Dr Banda act as a mediator between us and the President, but he also introduced us to other key Christian leaders in the country. By the time our Board of Trustees was formed we had developed friendships with outstanding men such as Jusaf Jaywayee (later to be Malawi's Ambassador to the United Nations), Pierson Chunga, Director of TransWorld Radio and Willie Musepole, a respected and active Christian businessman.

The biggest hurdle was being accepted by the CCAP (Central Church of Africa Presbyterian). This denomination, with over 800,000 members at that time, was almost a 'state church'. The President of Malawi himself had been an elder in the Scottish Presbyterian Church and strongly supported the CCAP denomination. We were able to set up meetings with the Nkoma Synod in the Central Region as well as in Blantyre (Southern Region) and the Livingstonia Synod in the north. Jack, being a Presbyterian (PCA) pastor, had the credibility necessary to gain their approval. But it was through the influence of the president, Kamuzu Banda himself, that the African Bible College received the document stating we were registered with the government as a *bona fide* mission organization, and accepted by the CCAP church.

It was not until our seventh trip across the continent of Africa from Liberia to Malawi that we brought our daughter Marion and her husband Steve Spencer and baby David with us. Their missionary career had begun in Liberia but we needed them along with Del, Becky, Paul and Laura to undertake the tremendous task of building the twenty buildings that the Missionary Tech Team in Longview, Texas had designed for this new college campus.

Jack and I had faced a multitude of disappointments as we sought out just the right piece of property. The 'planning department' of the city of Lilongwe vetoed every section of land we selected and Jack almost gave up several times. But as we prayed and waited on the Lord for His choice, the perfect location opened up. Sometimes God tests our seriousness by giving us the opportunity to persevere in spite of difficulties.

The African Bible College - Malawi was soon recognized by the government as a university-level college and it wasn't long before the fifty acre site was filled with a beautiful brick-built library, gymnasium, classrooms, chapel, dormitories and staff

Chapel in Malawi.

houses for the College. Paul began to have visions for even greater expansion and the African Bible College Christian Academy and the ABC Community Clinic were built on these manicured grounds. Little did we realize how effective the Christian Academy would become, with children from over thirty countries attending this educational institution. The ABC Clinic, which served the community and nearby village, became a source of security to the missionary staff and their children as well.

The African Bible College Compound, with its landscaped green grass, flowers and trees, is truly an oasis. It was Bart Bliss, when we presented the possibility of another college, who said, 'I believe the college in Malawi will be even bigger and better than the one here in Liberia!' He didn't know how prophetic that statement was to be! In William Carey's words, 'Thou shalt see greater things than these.'

34

'HONEY, WE NEED A RADIO STATION!'

We were flying over the Atlantic on our way to the States for furlough when I turned to Jack and said, 'Honey, we need our own radio station.' He looked at me in surprise but, without hesitation, he replied, 'We have enough projects to think about without getting into a radio station.' I went on to explain how important an instrument a radio station could be to our students, as well as the capital city of Lilongwe. The only broadcasting station in Malawi was the government's own one. Private licenses had not been given at that time. What an opportunity for a Christian broadcasting station! Not only that, but our Communication students needed the experience of actually being ON the air! When I did my training in Communication at Mississippi College, being 'on the air' was one thing that really helped to prepare me for broadcasting. But, as I could see that Jack wasn't interested in my latest 'brainstorm', I tactfully dropped the subject.

Our first missions' conference was at one of our favorite churches – the First Presbyterian Church in Macon, Georgia. We arrived there just in time for a dinner for visiting missionaries given in the home of one of the members. Before we could enjoy the delicious southern cooking, the phone rang. The call was for Jack, but the caller didn't even identify himself before he said, 'How would you like your own radio station?' Jack was literally speechless. He didn't know what to say. Finally he blurted out, 'That would be great, but we don't have money for a radio station!' The caller on the other end replied, 'Don't worry about the money. It's all taken care of.'

The amazing person on the phone was none other than Jim Lawhon. I don't think at that time he had a clue where the money was coming from, but as a missionary with HCJB (a Christian mission organization that helps set up radio stations around the world), he had a real burden for putting one in Malawi. So he did just that, or should I say that the Lord did just that!

We didn't know Jim Lawhon that well. His wife had recently passed away and we had known her as the manager of the Church's bookstore. There was also a strange connection ... the young man who had put his Faith into Action by giving his last ten dollars as a down payment for the gymnasium was Jim's wife's nephew!

'Honey, we need our own radio station,' was not just an idle comment made high over the Atlantic, it was a prompting from God Himself to help fulfill His Commission to get this Gospel into ALL the world. He had already laid the providential circumstances that would allow His command to be brought into being and He had prepared a lot of hearts to hear that command.

35

EVANGELISM EXPLOSION ON ABC CAMPUS IN MALAWI

'[God] sought for a man ... to stand in the gap ... but [He] found none.' (Ezek. 22:30 KJV) But then, there was Dr James Kennedy, pastor of the Coral Ridge Presbyterian Church in Fort Lauderdale, Florida. He was ready to fill in that *gap*. James Kennedy recognized the tremendous need for training the average 'church-goer' in the neglected skill of personal evangelism. The reluctance to talk to others about a 'personal relationship to Jesus Christ' was smothering the spiritual growth of many churches. Thus, he felt, that hole in the armor could be filled by evangelism – personal evangelism.

African Bible College in Liberia was opened in 1978. One of the courses required of all freshmen was 'personal evangelism'. Using the Navigator's course of Memorization of Scripture, this course became a foundation stone upon which all the other academic classes could build. Then, as the second African Bible College opened in Malawi, a Team of some thirty people came from the Coral Ridge Presbyterian Church to conduct EE Training Classes. Immediately, there was an affinity between the ABC students and the instructors training them in the principles and practices of Evangelism Explosion.

John Sorensen, (later to become President of EE) and Kirby Williams, a photographer with an amazing insight in producing a video that could be used over and over again in the promotion of African Bible College and EE as well, led the Team.

The impact was unparalled. Students at African Bible College became zealous and confident as soul-winners; EE Trainers were encouraged as they watched their protégés at work; the Coral Ridge Church and James Kennedy rejoiced as they heard testimonies and watched films of the results of this venture. In fact, when Dr Kennedy gave the address at PCA General Assembly, he showed Kirby William's videotape of the amazing response to EE's Training Session in Malawi.

As a result, African Bible College-Malawi instigated a new required course in its curriculum: Evangelism Explosion Training. It was quite natural, then, that God began to lay upon the heart of John Sorensen, now president of EE, the need for permanent Training Centers in Africa. And why not on the campus of the African Bible College in Malawi? Nevertheless, it was to take the providence of God to bring about this Partnership.

Jack and I always look forward when we are home in Jackson, Mississippi, to visiting 'my' church: the First Presbyterian Church in Jackson. So often, we are traveling and speaking in different churches, but the times we can attend the services at 'First Church' are very special to us. So, on this one particular Sunday evening after the worship service, we were enjoying the fellowship and talking to friends when suddenly, Jim Stuart (who had been the missions pastor at the church) came up to us and said, ' I am now with EE, and John Sorensen has been trying to get in touch with Jack or Paul'.

He went on to explain the plan that John had to build EE Training Centers throughout the world. There were already several in operation but he had a particular burden for Africa and he wanted to present a plan for EE to partner with African Bible College so they could put Training Centers on our campuses ... in Malawi, Uganda and Liberia.

The providence of God was apparent to me immediately! The next day was our annual Board Meeting. If we could get the information and the details right away, we could present this proposal at the Board Meeting! Early the next morning, we were able to get in touch with John Sorenson when he communicated to us his desire to establish the next Training Center in Malawi on the campus of African Bible College.

Thus, the agreement was made; plans were drawn up and presented to both the EE Board and the ABC Board of Directors. Construction began, and the EE Building (Lecture Hall and Dormitories) were dedicated in September 2011.

The bronze plaque on the front of the building reads:

Dedicated in honor of Dr D. James Kennedy, pastor, teacher, mentor, and founder of Evangelism Explosion International. Dr Kennedy was committed to training leaders to share the Gospel of Jesus Christ and equip others to do the same. In 1996 Evangelism Explosion became the first Christian ministry to be launched into every nation on earth. Each year, through the ministry, millions of people come to faith in Jesus Christ, all building on a vision Dr Kennedy received from Jeremiah 33:3, 'Call unto me and I will answer thee, and show thee great and mighty things which thou knowest not.' After reading this, he proclaimed to his congregation, 'We can change the world!' This training hall is dedicated to training and equipping 'World Changers.'

And so, one more building has been added to the African Bible College Campus in Malawi. Not merely one more building, but one more avenue for reaching the lost in Africa and one more means of accomplishing the philosophy of African Bible Colleges which is based on the firm belief that 'quality education with God's Word at the center cannot fail to produce quality leaders (world changers!) for Christ'.

36

THE PEARL OF AFRICA

A check fell unexpectedly out of an envelope. The amount overwhelmed us. We were even more surprised when we read the accompanying note: 'This is to buy the property you need to build another African Bible College in Uganda.'

Jack and I were once again on furlough and staying in the mission apartment of the Reformed Seminary in Jackson, Mississippi. We had been doing deputation in our supporting churches and had talked about the need for a Bible college in Uganda. At one church there was a young couple who had spent some time with the Peace Corps in Uganda and God had laid it on their hearts to give this huge gift to buy the land we would need to build the college.

The need for a college was becoming clearer and clearer as students from Uganda flooded the college in Malawi. We were impressed with the caliber of young people who so desperately wanted this kind of education that they traveled hundreds of miles to come to a Bible College in a totally different culture and country. Jack and I had been to Kampala several times to give the entrance exam and we were captivated by the progressiveness of this nation. The city of Kampala bustled with entrepreneurs from all parts of Africa and Europe. 'Boda bodas' (motor bikes) and bicycles zipped in and out of the congested traffic. Cars and buses were filled with people. And multitudes walked on the crowded roads, making it almost impossible to get through the roundabouts that led to Kampala. Even though there seemed to be an overabundance of so called 'colleges and universities',

African Bible College could meet a need for the kind of Christian higher education not being offered in this 'Pearl of Africa'.

Yet again the search for just the right piece of property began. Jack and I had no idea that this was to be a long and arduous task. We needed help and it came in the form of John Mpyisi. Mr Mpyisi had been Minister of Labor before the days of Idi Amin. It was necessary for him to go into exile during that time and he returned to re-establish his home after those years of terror. He was still a valuable cog in the wheel of the economic structure of Uganda. It was through his many colleagues and contacts that we were able to walk just about every available piece of land in Kampala, Entebbe and their surrounding areas! Nothing seemed just right. We made trip after trip, each time becoming more discouraged. We even took Marion and Steve on one of those visits to see if they could help us find land suitable for the college.

A beautiful piece of property on the outskirts of Kampala seemed perfect. There was only one problem – it was not available. On our seventh trip, as Jack and I sat on a Sunday morning in the packed Anglican church, I was looking through my Bible waiting for the service to begin when the words of Psalm 121 leaped out at me. 'I will lift up mine eyes to the hills – from whence cometh my help?' (NKJV). I leaned over and showed it to my husband (who doesn't like me to talk in church), and whispered; 'Lubowa Hills.' This was the unavailable property I had set my heart on. After the service I suggested, 'Let's go out to Lubowa Hills this afternoon and just walk around.' Jack's answer was an emphatic, 'I'm not wasting my time doing that. You know it's not for sale.'

As a good wife, I was silent ... but prayed he would change his mind! Later that afternoon Jack started putting on his 'old' shoes. I asked, 'What are you doing?' 'Didn't you say you wanted to go out to Lubowa Hills?' he answered. That Sunday afternoon we walked 'our' property. The next morning Jack reluctantly called the realtor and was embarrassed even to ask if the property were by any chance available for sale. It was a shock when the voice on the other end said, 'Yes, it has just opened up. Can you meet me there in an hour?'

Not only was the 'perfect' land open to us but, because it was owned by someone in Britain and it was the last of the 'free-holder's land', African Bible College was allowed to purchase it instead of leasing, as is usually the procedure in Africa. The Pearl of Africa had just added another jewel to her string of pearls, a new institution of higher learning to train Christian leaders to meet the need of this booming, beautiful country.

My brother, Palmer Robertson, author and scholar, agreed to head up this college in Uganda and he and his wife Joanna have been exactly the right team to meet the challenges of establishing a university in Africa.

Waiting on God is never easy. Elijah had to go look for that rain seven times. Joshua had to march his people around the walls of Jericho seven times. And Jack and I made seven trips to Uganda searching for the land God had promised us. This is another example of the motto for African Bible College: Faith in action – God in motion.

The African Bible College Chapel on the campus of the college in Uganda.

37

THE BIRTH OF A STATION

'Radio ABC 99.3 FM is on the air!' The birth of the radio station in Uganda was somewhat dramatic. Jack and I were in Uganda on the campus of the new African Bible College waiting at the radio station – one of the most finely equipped stations in all of Africa – for the Inspector from the Broadcasting Council of Uganda to arrive. With us were two Ugandan graduates of ABC Malawi, Linda Owar and Rachel Ainebyoni, who were going to be the station operators. Also there were Rob Branch and his assistant, Curtis Young, Kenny Mackenzie (our Scottish building supervisor) and my brother Palmer along with Mr and Mrs Mpyisi, our Ugandan Board member and friend, and McCloud Munthali, station manager from the radio station in Malawi.

Rob Branch, the engineer from the States, and I had spent hours preparing all the documents needed to apply for the radio license, and the day before we carefully went over all the requirements to make certain we were ready for the inspection. Rob had even purchased a filter at the last minute before leaving Virginia because it was on the list of stipulated equipment. Not only was the filter expensive but it was also huge and so formidable looking that he was afraid it would arouse suspicion at the airport. I suggested he buy a golf bag to put it in but, when he went to the sports store, he found a double gun case that was just perfect! And, as it was 'airport approved' he was able to check it in without difficulty.

At 10 o'clock sharp – the appointed time for the inspection – the Broadcasting Council van with all the electronic testing equipment arrived at the ABC gate. The guard ran before the van to take it directly to the studio. When I saw there were only two men inside, my heart fell. We had expected a much larger delegation of important officials. I had even asked Joanna to have tea for them after the Inspection was over. What a disappointment!

The technical engineer jumped out of the van and went straight to work. He and Rob Branch had their own electronic engineering language and that's what they spoke as the inspector went from place to place – testing this, examining that – and we all followed. Finally, when he reached the 210 ft. tower and was checking his GPS sightings, I said, 'Is everything all right?' When the response was positive, I was encouraged to ask the next question, 'Can we go on the air?'

His answer was, 'Usually we have tests for three weeks.' I responded quickly, 'Mr Bantuluki said that if everything was all right we could go on the air tomorrow. And,' I said confidently, 'everything is perfect!' He ran back to his van, turned on our station and it was clear as a bell. 'Your modulation is two per cent off' he said. Rob quickly rushed into the studio, made the adjustment, and the inspector was satisfied. Radio ABC 99.3 FM was on the air! As he climbed into the van, he nodded his head and said, 'You may stay on the air!' It had all happened so quickly that we stood there – stunned! He didn't even stay for tea! I said to Jack later, 'I think he was an angel!' Rob Branch remarked that he had never worked with such an efficient and cooperative inspector.

Was it really that easy? How did it happen that African Bible Colleges now had three radio stations operating? It all began when Ed Ingels encouraged me to become a Ham operator. He promised to buy the radio, tower and all the equipment needed if I would work to get a license. That seemed impossible: to send and receive the Morse Code at 15 words per minute; to learn multitudes of algebraic formulas; to learn the lingo of electrical engineering. But I was motivated. At that time Jack and I were in Liberia but the twins were in college at Biola University;

Marion was in boarding school in Ivory Coast and Lisa was in California getting serious with some young man we didn't even know. So, I became a Ham operator – EL8J in Liberia and later 7Q7Nc in Malawi.

But even before that, Bart Bliss left his position with ELWA (the SIM Mission radio station in Monrovia) to come with African Bible College in Yekepa to instigate a Communication program. The training was so successful that ELWA was happy to receive our graduates on their radio staff. It was this success, and the recognition of the tremendous need for trained broadcasters in Africa, that inspired me to say to Jack on that airplane as we flew to the States with the vision for the second Bible College in Malawi, 'Honey, we need a radio station.' In God's providence, it was only a short time later that Jim Lawhon called us while we were at a missions' conference with the question, 'How would you like your own radio station in Malawi?'

As a result, Radio ABC 88.3Fm was the first radio station to be established in the country of Malawi other than the government operated one. We have since trained hundreds of young people in broadcasting. Many now have key positions in radio and television throughout Malawi. One is even an announcer for the BBC in London.

The station in Uganda has the same amazing story. On December 12, 2001 Paul was with us in Uganda as we were seeking permission to open a new radio station in Kampala. I remember he stayed up all night finishing the correspondence with the Broadcasting Commission. He even wrote Mr Bantuluki requesting that he reserve the frequency 87.5 FM for Radio ABC. We completed all the application forms and felt that all the bases had been covered. But in 2005, when we were actually ready to ship over all the equipment, we were told that we now needed to complete a fifty-page book, thirty-five bound copies to be submitted to the Broadcasting Council. Shortly after that Paul called from Uganda and reported that the President had issued an ultimatum. 'No more radio stations were to be established in Uganda.'

But we were NOT NEW! As I talked to the Chairman of the Broadcasting Commission on the telephone from Malawi I reminded him that our initial application was made on July 29, 1999! In God's Providence, he was (as he himself put it) a 'born again' Christian and gave us permission to install the radio equipment with its 210 ft. tower.

The Christian Mission HCJB sent two tower builders – a husband and wife team, Jean and Ed Muehlfelt. Jean came from a family of tower builders and was up and down the tower as much as her husband. The last thing to be done was to put on the red and white paint. The day of the inspection the paint was still not dry – but they made it!

After the station in Uganda was approved and Radio ABC 99.3FM was officially on the air, we had one last concern. The two graduates, Linda and Rachel, were overwhelmed with the responsibility of a seventeen-hour day of broadcasting. A phone call was made to another graduate who lived over eight hours away and he agreed to make the trip to Kampala. As we finished our prayer meeting that night at Palmer and Joanna's house, there was a knock on the door. Just as when Peter came unexpectedly to the prayer meeting in the book of Acts, we could hardly believe that our new 'station manager' was standing outside the door! I said, 'Why did you come?' He answered, 'My heart brought me!'

Surely only God Himself could have orchestrated such amazing providences to bring these stations into being. Though we know that Satan is the 'prince of the power of the air', we are penetrating his territory with the sharp and powerful two-edged sword of the Word of God.

38

THE TOO-A-LOO BIRD IS SINGING AGAIN!

The love affair that began with Liberia before we ever touched those shores did not wane or falter during all the fifteen years of war and turmoil. Every time there was a lull in the fighting, I would say to Jack, 'Let's go back!' His answer was invariably, 'It's not time yet'.

The first evacuation of the College, when we fled over the Guinea border, barely escaping the flying bullets of the rebel invasion of Yekepa, was in the spring of 1990. Charles Taylor and his troops occupied the city and held much of the territory outside Monrovia. It was during this time that Jack, Glenn Byerly and Bob Branch decided to make an attempt to go inside the rebel-held territory and rescue some of the documents left in the offices. They also wanted to try to meet with the rebel commanders to see if they would allow us to send in missionaries and re-open the College. It was a bold venture, but these three men were veteran missionaries with years of experience of being a part of the African culture. They felt the expedition would be safe.

I stayed behind in Ivory Coast in the border town of Danane with the other wives but gave Jack detailed instructions on where to find all the students' transcripts in the Registrar's office, as well as where to locate all my Bible College by Radio scripts and teaching notes. I don't think I realized that he would be looking through these files at night with a flashlight as there was no electricity in the entire city! Someone gave them a can of cranberry sauce as they drove off. It was to be their Thanksgiving dinner!

Jack also had a mandate from his granddaughters Sophie, Charisa, Joanna and Janell (Del and Becky's girls) to make sure to bring Benjy, our Golden Retriever, with them when they came back. When told we had to leave Benjy in Yekepa when we evacuated, the girls couldn't understand. Jack explained that we only had room for people in the crowded car, but the girls said, 'But, Grampy, Benjy IS PEOPLE!' So Jack had that responsibility as well.

The primary object of the trip was to see if it would be safe to re-open the African Bible College. Hence, as soon as the men reached their destination, Jack went down to the rebel headquarters in Yekepa and asked to meet with the Commanding Officer. His request was granted and he was immediately placed in a room surrounded by soldiers, all with AK-47s, and all looking very intimidating and serious. However, as he talked with the Commander, he was assured that Charles Taylor's rebels would give our missionaries protection and that we were free to re-open the African Bible College. Once again, mission accomplished!

The next day, as the men were loading the car to leave, limping up the college's palm tree-lined driveway came none other than our beloved dog, Benjy! He was thin and weak. His nose had been cut open by a cutlass, but he was still alive. Every other dog in the entire town of Yekepa had been eaten. During the height of the war there was a shortage of food for the people and the soldiers as well. In desperation, eating dogs became a means of sustaining life. However, our beautiful Benjy had been hidden by some friends who knew how much he meant to our family. Somehow Benji became aware that Jack was on the campus, and made his way to him. As Jack and the others knew that it was not safe to try to take a dog across the border, they tied him down to the floor on the back seat. They knew it was going to be difficult enough getting across the border with all they had rescued from the College without having a dog complicating things!

But God's providence was once again at work. As they drove through the village near the border, Jack spotted one of our former students, Thomas Gweh. He was dressed in a rebel Commander's uniform. They stopped the car and asked if he would go with them to the border. Thomas Gweh agreed and at each checkpoint simply waved his hand and the gates swung open wide for the car to pass untroubled through. Only once did a young soldier refuse but Thomas was out of the car in a flash and the young soldier was down on the ground doing push-ups!

It was this venture of faith that brought about the first re-opening of the Bible College in 1992. The college remained open until the Nigerian 'peace-keeping' force sent jets to fly over the city and the campus of African Bible College threatening to drop bombs, hoping to discourage Charles Taylor's troops. It was during this time that one of our missionaires, Glenn Byerly, dug 'fox holes' (such as the combat soldiers did during the war!) in his backyard. When the jets flew over he ran for cover, sometimes with his corn-bread from dinner still in his hands! When evacuation once again seemed inescapable, Fern and Glenn Byerly opened the African Bible College in Exile in the remote border town of Danane and for two years held classes in their home, often sacrificing their own food to feed the students who had no means of support.

Later, Del and Becky, with the Sarrets, reopened the College for almost a full year. When the school was finally forced to close many of the students lacked only nine weeks till their graduation! So it was that in 1995, Jack and I, with Steve Sarret and Carolyn and Bob Branch, went back to the border town of Danane and held classes that brought students from as far away as Ghana and Sierra Leone so they could finally graduate and receive their degree from African Bible College! When the Liberian national anthem was sung in the Mayor's Hall of Danane, there were hundreds of Liberians in exile singing loudly. I am sure they could be heard at heaven's doors. It was a glorious and victorious occasion. Those graduates were to become the Christian leaders who would help to bring Liberia back to the 'peaceful, happy land of glorious liberty by God's command' they were singing about in their national anthem.

For five years the grounds of the African Bible College remained untouched. One of our students from Ghana wrote us a letter during that period and said he had a dream in which he saw angels with flaming swords keeping watch over that campus. And then it was all gone. The looting, the desecration, and finally the ravages of the jungle consumed the buildings and soon even the paths and roads to the houses and buildings were so overgrown that, when we were able to make our way back into

Yekepa, we could not even find our house amidst all the vines that entangled it. What happened to those protecting angels? Maybe people forgot to pray. But perhaps God had a greater plan in bringing glory to Himself.

In this time of discouragement Jack was reminded of the promise of restoration in Jeremiah, the promise that God had given him the day he was forced to leave Yekepa. '"For I know the plans I have for you, plans for welfare and not for calamity to give you a future and a hope. Then you will call upon Me and come and pray to Me, and I will listen to you. You will seek Me and find Me, when you search for Me with all your heart. And I will be found by you," declares the LORD, "and I will restore your fortunes ..."' (29:11-14 NASB)

All through those long years of waiting, Jack preached that sermon over and over. It was entitled 'Our God is a God of restoration and when He restores, He makes it better than new.'

Could we believe that now ... as Del, Becky, Jack and I stood together, holding hands looking at the devastation? Could we covenant to return to this 'heap of rubble' and trust God to restore the African Bible College? Could we trust God alone and not wait for that powerful Iron Ore Company to return? Could we dare once again to put our faith into action and watch God go into motion?

We had only to bow our heads and tell Him we were willing to take that step of faith and He was ready to go to work! By the time we had driven the eight hours back to Monrovia, it was already announced on the radio that the huge iron ore corporation, Mittel Steel had signed a contract with the government to reopen the mine in Yekepa. Now all we needed was a plan. How on earth was this miracle of restoration to take place?

As we pondered how this could be accomplished, God brought to mind His great miracle of the restoration of the temple in Jerusalem following the Jews' seventy years of exile in the city of Babylon, and the miracle of God's raising up the great Persian King Cyrus to set God's people free and to encourage them to return to Jerusalem and restore the temple that lay in ruins. King Cyrus, after his amazing defeat of Babylon, announced to the Jews in captivity that God had appointed him to free them so they could return to Jerusalem to restore the temple. It was the Jews' response found in Ezra 1:5-7 that caught Jack's attention. 'Then the heads of fathers' *households* of Judah and Benjamin and the priests and the Levites arose, even everyone whose spirit God had stirred to go up and rebuild the house of the LORD which is in Jerusalem. All those about them encouraged them with articles of silver, with gold, with goods, with cattle and with valuables ...' (NASB).

EUREKA! There it was – God's plan for the restoration of the African Bible College. Jack called it the King Cyrus Plan. The plan was to challenge churches to restore the twenty-two buildings by sending out teams to rebuild. But more than that, each team was to be accompanied by a container that was filled, by those who stayed behind, with everything needed for the restoration of their building. In this way, the whole church would be involved as they gathered the materials needed. It worked. Churches had tremendous experiences both in gathering the supplies and through sending work teams to restore the buildings.

God had yet another miracle in store in order to fulfill His promise of Restoration – Samaritan's Purse.

While Del and Becky were attending LeTourneau College in Longview, Texas they became good friends with Franklin Graham, founder of Samaritan's Purse and son of the great evangelist, Billy Graham. Franklin Graham had actually become acquainted with African Bible College through his good friend and mentor, Roy Gustavson, and later, Dennis Agajanian, both of whom had visited the campus in Liberia. Soon after our evacuation and the rebel invasion of Yekepa Jack and I were asked by Dennis Agajanian to attend a crusade in California where Franklin was speaking. As soon as we were introduced to him, as he was heading for the platform to speak, he asked, 'What can we do to help?' We told him that all our vehicles had been taken over by the rebels and we had no way to travel back to the campus from Ivory Coast, if we were able to return. He answered right away, 'Go to the headquarters of Samaritan's Purse and they will help you.' We did, and they were able to help us get the vehicle we needed to drive to the campus.

When Franklin became aware of the number of our graduates who were working with Samaritan's Purse in Liberia, he recognized the need for African Bible College to be put back into operation in order to continue to supply the Christian leadership required to help restore that country. Del showed him a picture of the chapel on the campus; it was just a shell of a building. Franklin said, 'This pile of rubble is not glorifying to God.' At that moment, he made the decision to make the restoration of the African Bible College a prime ministry for Samaritan's Purse.

It was in that same chapel, beautifully restored, that the President of Liberia, Ellen Johnson Sirleaf, said, 'As we entered the African Bible College University campus, I felt a rush of adrenaline, a surge of excitement of what Liberia could become...' Her closing words were, 'This campus impresses upon us how restoration can transform.' Jack, Del and I had met President Sirleaf before we even began rebuilding the college. Then Jack presented her with a picture of what the College had looked like before the war, but now, truly, restoration was complete ... and better than new!

Yes, the too-a-loo bird is singing again. The motto of the small nation of Liberia is 'The love of liberty brought us here.' It was also love that moved us out of our comfort zone to a place we had never seen, yet somehow loved. It was surely the love of Christ for the lost and hurting that set us off on this 'Sentimental journey across Africa.'

President Ellen Johnson-Sirleaf on the day before her
inauguration as President of Liberia
L to R: Del, Nell, President Sirleaf; Jack and African Bible
College graduate, Richard Ballingar.

39

'God has done this'

The security was tight. The two Samaritan's Purse helicopters circled the African Bible College campus in Liberia and we watched in awe as they prepared to land on the field next to the new gymnasium. The helicopter blades stirred up the dust and the breeze so strongly that we ran for cover behind the building. Suddenly, the men were jumping out and running for the bus we had driven down to pick them up and take them to 'our' house. Yes, it was the house we thought would last forever but which had been totally destroyed during the war.

The house had been rebuilt by a team from The Grove Bible Church in Chandler, Arizona where our son Palmer was pastor. It was not really our home any more but was being used by Del and Becky as their 'home away from home'. Their home was actually in Kenya where Del was the head of the Theological Department at Daystar University and Becky began 'Amani Aju', a work intended to help refugee women from neighboring countries. Being herself a refugee from Liberia, Becky understood the emptiness of a displaced woman. 'The house that would last forever' was also being used to house the large number of teams that had flooded the African Bible College campus over the past several years.

Security was tightened even more the next day when Dr Franklin Graham himself landed in the Samaritan's Purse helicopter on the open field of the African Bible College campus. He had flown his own plane across the Atlantic Ocean to the small insignificant country of Liberia, not only to give the Dedication Message in the beautifully restored African Bible College Chapel, but also to give a series of Evangelistic messages in Monrovia at the huge football stadium. We later attended these meetings and were overwhelmed with the number of people who literally RAN forward to receive Christ when the invitation was given.

Franklin Graham as he gave the message at the African Bible College in
Liberia in the Restored ABC Chapel.
(Courtesy of Samaritan's Purse)

The King Cyrus Plan had truly been God's plan for rebuilding the African Bible College. Church after church sent teams in response to our plea to restore the college which had been destroyed by the Civil War. Now it was all put back together again ... better than before! We were gathered to dedicate, or as Franklin Graham said in his message at the Dedicatory Service, 'to re-dedicate' the beautifully, miraculously restored African Bible College UNIVERSITY. Cameramen, journalists, members of the Billy Graham Association and the Samaritan's Purse all were there to surround Franklin Graham with their assistance and protection. We were there to rejoice and see what God had done.

Franklin Graham had seen the pictures. He knew what the college campus had looked like after fifteen years of war.

Not only had the jungle recaptured the entire grounds and buildings, but the elements and looting had left only empty shells of the buildings that had once graced that beautiful campus. 'God has done this,' Franklin said, in his address to the students, the members of government and other officials. 'It is a miracle!'

Providentially, Dennis Agajanian was there with the team, playing his guitar. We had truly come full circle. Dennis was in Yekepa just weeks before the rebel invasion. He had come to the College with Roy Gustafson, (a pastor with the Billy Graham Association) who was instrumental in bringing Franklin through his 'rebel' years and turning him into a valiant warrior for God. Dennis was back in Liberia and the people loved him.

Known as the 'fastest guitar-playing dirt bike rider in the world,' Dennis's unusual talents were used to rescue me in a time of dire need – and I wasn't in need of fast guitar playing! While he was visiting the ABC campus some time earlier, I fell over cracks in the sidewalk at the post office and came crying home with all my front teeth broken, mouth bleeding and looking like I had been in the ring with a prize fighter. Dennis took one look at me and said he would drive me to the dentist at ELWA in Monrovia. 'It's too late,' I said, 'he doesn't stay after 4:30.' It was at least a four or five hour drive and, even under the best conditions, I knew we couldn't make it. But Dennis and Palmer insisted I lie down in the back seat of our new Peugeot and with Dennis flying over those dirt roads he lived up to his reputation, and there I was safely in the dentist's chair getting my front teeth repaired before he finished for the day! After we were all evacuated from Yekepa, Dennis offered his condo in California to Veronica and Palmer until they could find somewhere to live. Dennis was one of those people that shine like a star in a dark night and the war allowed us to see that.

There is no doubt that God wanted African Bible College restored. I often reflect on the beginning of that 'impossible dream' and the part that Del and Becky played in its realization. Our first thought as we began to plan for the building of that college, was to have Del come to Liberia and take over the construction. It was a very logical plan. He was attending LeTourneau College at the time and was about to graduate with a degree in Missionary Technology! He had even been taught how to build with cement block! So, a letter went flying across the ocean saying, 'Come over and help us!' The reply came back, 'I'm sorry, Mom and Dad, but at this time I have no heart for missions.' I couldn't believe it! So, I sat right down and wrote him this poem:

An aerial view of the restored chapel.

NO HEART FOR MISSIONS?
My son, how can this be?
When His own Heart was broken
For you, on Calvary.

NO HEART FOR MISSIONS?
When every moment millions die
And enter dark eternity
To gnash their teeth and cry.

NO HEART FOR MISSIONS?
Is no heart for Christ,
For His very Heartbeat stopped
To pay the awful price.

NO HEART FOR MISSIONS?
No life to live for Him?
T'will be an empty feeling
When the world begins to dim
And the things that stole your heart
No longer seem fulfilling.

When the glitter of their spark
Has tarnished with the living,
And your heart cries out again
Too late. The time is finished,
The harvest is counted in.

My prayer for you, my Son
On your Graduation Day,
Is that God will give you a burning heart
And you will know no rest
Until your feet have turned
To follow in HIS WAY.

Needless to say, Del and Becky's feet did turn to Africa, where they have been serving the Lord over thirty years, where they have raised four daughters and have built the African Bible College ... twice!

There's an old proverb that says, 'The proof is in the pudding', and that is so true of African Bible College. The hundreds of graduates have proven the value of the education they received, by the way they shone like stars during those dark and dismal days of civil war. They were not only faithful to God in their places of leadership, even as exiles in foreign lands, but some of them remained in Liberia in spite of the danger to their lives in order to keep the Gospel alive. And when those who left returned, they were ready to serve and to lead their country back to stability as they took on positions of leadership.

The Bible College in Liberia is not alone in the impact it has had on the continent of Africa. The College in Malawi (now with over 600 graduates spread across East Africa) and the graduates of the College in Uganda reaching into Central and northern Africa, have confirmed that the vision God gave to Jack under the Indian almond tree was indeed God's answer to the question we faced in the jungles of Liberia: 'Where are all these young people going when they complete high school?'

The answer to that question – Bible colleges scattered over Africa – producing jewels to make us His crown!

PART VII

WHAT'S NEXT? – GOD'S PLAN FOR AFRICA INCLUDES US!

40

GONE WITH THE WIND

This story of the Yankee Officer and the Southern Belle began on the beautiful Gulf Coast of Mississippi the day that young Naval Officer came to call on the one he would later call 'My Nell'. Lulu and Owen Palmer (my grandparents) were sitting out on the front lawn of their beautiful home overlooking the beach and water from the Gulf of Mexico, enjoying the cool ocean breeze and the afterglow from the setting sun, unaware that life would never be the same again for the granddaughter they loved so much. History was in the making. The combination of these two young people, later to become united with a Third, was to change the face of an entire continent.

Little did we realize then that all that beauty, all that serenity, would not last forever. Sixty years later it was all gone just like Tara in *Gone with the Wind*. Hurricane Katrina completely blew away that beautiful home on 1308 East Beach in Gulfport, Mississippi, and with that wind went a lot of memories. But it also brought home a strong reminder that the things of this earth are temporal. Nothing will last forever.

How many times does God have to tell me that? The fire in Liberia that destroyed our bamboo house; the second fire a year later that ravished our two-story cement block house that I was certain would last forever; the loss of our home and Bible college in the rebel invasion in Yekepa – each of these was God's way of impressing upon me that this world is not my home. Nevertheless, it was painful to realize that the place which held so many precious memories was 'Gone with the Wind'.

Recently someone remarked that it was such a waste that all that money that had been invested in the buildings of African Bible College in Liberia was now gone. But it has not gone. The buildings were just a means to an end. Fifteen years of training students, of teaching the Word of God, of being a channel for God to use to send missionaries was certainly not a waste. Investment in LIVES is never a waste.

And as we build Bible Colleges across this unstable, volatile African Continent, we are not considering the cost if the buildings do not last forever. We are building men and women for eternity. They will last forever.

Although where it all began on the beautiful gulf coast of Mississippi is now gone with the wind, there is already a new beginning. The new generation – our children and our grandchildren – are falling in love with the same Person who has inspired us and challenged us to trust him for greater and greater steps of faith across the African Continent.

The love affair that began with the Yankee Officer and the Southern Belle is still alive. The magnolias have not wilted, the mint juleps have not melted and that dashing Naval Officer in his sparkling white uniform still puts stars in the eyes of his Nell.

When God told Abraham to go to that unknown place, He promised to give him as many descendants as the stars in the sky. We, too, followed God into the unknown and our spiritual children, grandchildren and great grandchildren are too numerous to count. We continue to enlarge the place of our tent and to strengthen our stakes with the Gospel going out all across Africa over Radio ABC and African Bible Colleges' graduates preaching and teaching God's Word throughout this vast continent. He is indeed multiplying the seed that was planted that summer on the seawall of the Gulf Coast, under that Mississippi moonlit sky.

The Yankee Officer and the Southern Belle

Christian Focus Publications
publishes books for all ages

Our mission statement –

STAYING FAITHFUL
In dependence upon God we seek to impact the world through literature faithful to His infallible Word, the Bible. Our aim is to ensure that the Lord Jesus Christ is presented as the only hope to obtain forgiveness of sin, live a useful life and look forward to heaven with Him.

REACHING OUT
Christ's last command requires us to reach out to our world with His gospel. We seek to help fulfil that by publishing books that point people towards Jesus and help them develop a Christ-like maturity. We aim to equip all levels of readers for life, work, ministry and mission.

Books in our adult range are published in three imprints:

Christian Focus contains popular works including biographies, commentaries, basic doctrine and Christian living. Our children's books are also published in this imprint.

Mentor focuses on books written at a level suitable for Bible College and seminary students, pastors, and other serious readers. The imprint includes commentaries, doctrinal studies, examination of current issues and church history.

Christian Heritage contains classic writings from the past.

Christian Focus Publications Ltd,
Geanies House, Fearn, Ross-shire,
IV20 1TW, Scotland, United Kingdom.
www.christianfocus.com